# YOUR PERSONALITY AND YOU

Dr. Splaver, a counseling psychologist, discusses personality. What is it? Are you born with it? Do you develop it? Can you change it? In her book she helps a young person understand why he behaves the way he does and she covers such subjects as home environment and family relationships; your very important brain; you and your emotions; your conscious and unconscious approaches to problems; what maturity really means, etc. She emphasizes the need for communication between young people and their parents, for their mutual good, and stresses the fact that people *can* change. A very important and helpful book for young people growing up in today's complex world.

*Books by Sarah Splaver*

**YOUR CAREER—IF YOU'RE NOT GOING TO COLLEGE**

**YOUR COLLEGE EDUCATION—HOW TO PAY FOR IT**

**YOUR PERSONALITY AND YOU**

# YOUR
# PERSONALITY
# AND YOU

by
## SARAH SPLAVER, Ph.D.

**JULIAN MESSNER**
**NEW YORK**

Published by Julian Messner
Division of Pocket Books, Inc.
8 West 40 Street, New York 10018

Printed in the United States of America
Library of Congress Catalog Card No. 65-22251

To

my brother-in-law

LEONARD ROSALSKY, M.D.

# CONTENTS

## Contents

## Contents

Contents

# 1

# PUTTING ON AN ACT

YOU ARE UNIQUE. ONLY YOU ARE JUST LIKE YOU. There is no one else exactly like you in this whole wide world. (And this holds true even if you are an identical twin.) There is only one of you out of 3,500,000,000 people on this earth, and that does make you someone special.

You ARE different. But, despite your differences, you have a great deal in common with these billions of other human beings who populate our planet. You think, you feel, you reason, you remember. These other people do too. You want to be liked. These other people do too. To be liked, you must be able to get along well with others. Here, so many people have problems.

Mastering the ability to get along with each other is probably one of the most difficult things for people to accomplish. So much unpleasantness, so much hardship, so many of the difficulties of life result from the inability to do this. On the large-scale international level, wars result because of this inability. On the family level, broken homes result. On the small-scale interpersonal level, people battle and bicker and squabble because of this inability to get along with others.

Let me give you a case in point: As I walked up the steps leading to the entrance of a city high school recently, I met two dejected students. Jimmy's lips were tight with anger. Alice's face looked flushed and fatigued. We stopped to chat and Jimmy told me his tale of woe.


## THE TALE OF THE TENDER TEN

Jimmy had accepted the task of producing a special class performance. Nine of his classmates had volunteered to join him in this project. The first meeting of the group had been called for this afternoon.

Thus, *ten young people had gathered in a room.*

In front of the room, leaning against the teacher's desk stood Jimmy, the project chairman. Alice, his assistant, stood passively alongside him as several students' strident voices filled the air.

Her nostrils constricted with anger, Susie snarled at Jimmy, "Why must things be done your way? I say my ideas are much better. I think you're just trying to be a dictator."

Cathy, who amply filled the school chair, cautiously came to Jimmy's defense. "I think Jimmy's right. As chairman, it's up to him to say what should be done."

Frankie bellowed in a loud bass voice, "Everybody has the right to say what should be done."

"Of course, everybody has that right," echoed Nancy, Frankie's "steady." Then, as an afterthought, she added, "Frankie has some good ideas too and we need good ideas here."

Charlie, who commanded everyone's respect and admiration because he is a member of the football team, suggested, "How about some teamwork and some cooperation. That's what we need here more than anything else. This is a group project, so let's act like a group."

"Yes, that's exactly what I say," agreed Susie, as she resumed her favorite theme. "I'm part of this group, so let's work on my ideas. They're good ones."

Alice flared at Susie. "Oh, you don't want any teamwork. You just want to have your way."

Standing near the window was Eddie, working conscientiously on the removal of a spot of dirt on his shirt, but his ears were keenly attuned to everything being said in the room. Looking up at Jimmy, he said, "I don't care whose ideas you accept. If we don't do things perfectly, the way they should be done, it will all be a waste. If we're going to do things like a bunch of amateurs, it's all not worth doing."

"Oh, Mr. Perfection himself," sneered Susie.

In the last row of seats sat Billy, a very unassuming, short, slender young man. No one paid any attention to him. He apparently found the bickering rather embarrassing, and so he slipped silently and slowly out of his seat and left.

*Ten young people had gathered in a room. Now there were nine.*

The wrangling continued with strident voices resounding throughout the room. Jimmy had been trying hard to be fair to each one in the group and to listen quietly and indulgently to each suggestion, but soon he lost his patience and shouted, "Nobody can hear what anybody is saying with everybody talking at the same time. So, all of you—shut up!"

This order produced the desired effect. Suddenly all was quiet, except for the tattoo which Frankie's fingers were playing on the arm of his chair. Frankie stretched his gangling legs. The high school chairs were quite inadequate for his six-foot frame. He rose, removed a cigarette from his pocket and placed it unlit in his mouth.

Cathy stared at him disapprovingly. "You'll get us into trouble, Frankie. You're not allowed to smoke in this room."

The cigarette hung limply from Frankie's lips. He was silent for a moment. Then, taking the cigarette from his mouth, he looked at Cathy, pointed the cigarette at her and said, "Cathy, if you didn't eat so much, you wouldn't be so fat. And, if you weren't so fat, you might even look pretty."

Cathy's lower lip started to quiver. Her eyes filled with tears. She rose and hurried out of the room.

*Ten young people had gathered in a room. Now there were eight.*

Jimmy shook his head angrily. "Now why did you have to say that?"

"Well, I didn't start it. She did."

Charlie mimicked his classmate, " 'I didn't start it. She did.' Good gosh, you sound like my little kindergarten cousin. Be a man. Go out and apologize to her. And, ask her to come back."

Nancy came to Frankie's defense. "Why should he! It was all her fault. Who is she to criticize Frankie for smoking? She didn't stop eating peanuts from the minute she came in here."

At the window side of the room, Eddie stopped trying to remove the dirt speck on his shirt and said, "There's no law against eating peanuts. But, there is a law against smoking."

Doleful Dolores had been daydreaming throughout the meeting, happily visualizing her part in the project. The attack on Cathy brought her back to reality. Full of sympathy for Cathy, she stared sternly at Frankie and said, "It wasn't necessary to be insulting. Cathy's sensitive about her weight, and you know it."

"Oh, come on. What are you people doing? Ganging up on me?" demanded Frankie furiously. "All of you know she eats too much and that she's too fat. That's why she doesn't really belong in this project."

"I'm the chairman and I'll decide who belongs here, without any help from you." Jimmy punctuated each word for emphasis.

Charlie, who is just as tall as Frankie, but more solidly built, rose, approached his classmate and said, "You know, you can be pretty nasty when you want to be. Cathy's eating has nothing to do with this project. And, if she eats too much, well, you smoke too much." Turning to Jimmy, he suggested, "Why don't we get on with trying to start this project going."

"Go ahead and work on your stupid project," jeered Frankie, "but without me."

As he turned to leave, he ordered Nancy, "Come on."

Alice looked fiercely at Frankie, "There's nothing stupid about this project. Jimmy knows exactly what he's doing."

Frankie ignored Alice, opened the door wide and left.

*Ten young people had gathered in a room. Now there were seven.*

Nancy followed after Frankie, but as she reached the door, she turned and scoffed at Alice, "Snob! If you want to blame this project's failure on somebody, don't blame Frankie. Blame Charlie and Jimmy and Eddie and Dolores—and yourself." After emphasizing the last word, Nancy left the room, closing the door behind her.

*Ten young people had gathered in a room. Now there were six.*

Jimmy placed his hand on Alice's shoulder. "Don't let her bother you. If she didn't have somebody to blame, her day would be spoiled."

Susie placed her well-chewed pencil in the small receptacle on the desk. "This whole project is falling apart. Let's admit it," she announced loudly. She turned to Alice. "I gave you such wonderful ideas on how we should do this. And, you paid no attention. Now, look what's happened."

Alice stared at Jimmy hoping for support. When none was forthcoming, she turned to Susie, shrugged her shoulders sheepishly, and said, "Well, it was not up to me to accept your ideas."

"It was up to Jimmy. And, you could have made him accept them."

"I could have?" asked Alice in disbelief.

Eddie, having finally succeeded in removing the difficult stain, left the window, returned to the center of the room, and approached Susie. "Susie, this is a group project, as Charlie said before. It wasn't just Jimmy. The whole group didn't go for your ideas. We've got to work together on something that's acceptable to everybody."

"Don't forget too," interjected Charlie, "it's the chairman who carries the chief responsibility for the project. If something goes wrong, Jimmy is the one who will be held accountable, not any of us. So, he should have more of the final say than any other member of the group."

"All right, enough of this," ordered Jimmy trying to regain control. "Let's see if those of us who are here can still get something done this afternoon."

Charlie glanced at his watch. "Sorry, Jimmy, but I've got to go. We wasted so much time arguing, I'm late for team practice."

Gloom set in over the remainder of the group. Charlie was highly regarded by his classmates. Without Charlie, the meeting appeared to be really doomed.

Alice asked hopefully, "Must you go? Stay for another half hour."

"I'd like to, Alice. I mean it. But, I've got three minutes to get to the gym, and the coach likes us to be on time. Let's try for a second meeting next week. Maybe we'll do better then."

Charlie hesitated for a moment and then added prudently, "Let's ask a faculty adviser to help us. We've got problems and I think we could use some good guidance." With that, he left.

*Ten young people had gathered in a room. Now there were five.*

Susie had heard enough. "Well, I don't think anyone here knows what he's doing. I'm going too."

As she started to leave, Jimmy begged, "Hold it, Susie. Just because Charlie had to go doesn't mean we're going to break up the meeting. We can still try to accomplish something."

Susie became incensed at the insinuation. "My leaving has nothing to do with Charlie's leaving. I gave you several good ideas. You didn't like them. The only thing you accomplished was a lot of fighting."

"Why do you have to get so emotional?" asked Alice perplexedly.

Susie's eyes glared as she shouted, "I'm not emotional!" With that, she turned and hurried out of the room.

*Ten young people had gathered in a room. Now there were four.*

"This is getting to be a really successful meeting," Eddie said with obvious sarcasm.

From the center of the room came Dolores' dejected voice. "That's exactly the way I feel," she said, which was an interesting comment, for Dolores had offered no suggestions and added little to the meeting. "I never did think this project would work," she added.

A tinge of anger was apparent in Jimmy's voice as he asked, "If that's what you thought, Dolores, then why did you join?"

"I'm interested in the project. I think it's a good thing. I hoped it would turn out all right. But, I wasn't optimistic about it."

As she stooped to gather up her books, her long black hair fell over her eyes. She straightened up again, announced, "I'm going home," then walked slowly to the door, turned the knob and left.

*Ten young people had gathered in a room. Now there were three.*

Eddie smiled as he remarked, "She 'wasn't optimistic about it.' Hah! She 'wasn't optimistic'!"

He started to laugh, causing Alice to do the same.

"She 'wasn't optimistic,'" he repeated. "That's the overstatement of the year. That girl is a perpetual picture of pessimism. When she gets up in the morning, it must come as a shock to her to discover that the world is still here."

Alice stopped laughing and looked at Eddie pensively. "Sometimes I feel that way too, so I can understand how Dolores feels."

It was Jimmy who was truly deep in the doldrums. "I'm glad you stopped laughing, because I don't see anything funny. We had such big plans. We were going to do this all by ourselves. We were going to prove to the faculty that we could do it without their assistance. Now, what do we do?"

Meekly, Alice replied, "What do we do? Let's give up. I think I'll go home too."

Jimmy found it hard to control his anger. "Fine. Go home. But first, tell me, how does your giving up differ from Susie's? You were so annoyed when she left."

Alice wrinkled her nose and half-closed her eyes. She could see no similarity between herself and Susie. "Susie left because she couldn't have her way. I stayed."

"Thanks," said Jimmy. "You're supposed to be my assistant. I asked you to assist me, in case you've forgotten."

"I haven't forgotten, Jimmy. I tried hard. But, what could I have done that I didn't do?"

Eddie eyed her sympathetically. "I'm sorry, Alice, but I've got to say this. I don't think you tried hard enough." Turning to Jimmy, he added, "And you too, Jimmy. You're the chairman. You should be the leader. You're supposed to keep the group together."

These words might have irked Jimmy had they come from some-one else. But he knew that Eddie was trying to be constructive. "All right, what didn't I do that I should have done?"

With the pencil with which he had been toying, Eddie pointed to the back of the room. "Well, for example," he said, "I saw that new fellow Billy come in and sit down quietly back there. He wanted to cooperate on this project. Nobody spoke to him. No one made him feel welcome."

"I didn't see him come in," insisted Jimmy. "But, since you did, why didn't you welcome him?"

"Because, like everyone else here, I suppose I was too involved in my own ideas about how things should be done. But, you're the one who's running the show. You, or Alice, should have ap-proached him."

There was a look of earnest surprise on Alice's face. "Honestly, Eddie. I didn't see him come in. I didn't know he was here."

"I guess you're right, Eddie," Jimmy agreed. "Billy told me in our math class this morning that he wanted to join. I said we'd be glad to have him. But instead of being the leader, I was so busy acting as referee with all the battling going on here that I just didn't notice him."

"And another thing you should have done," continued Eddie.

"You should have given more attention to Cathy's idea at the beginning of the meeting. I think it was good."

Alice arched her left eyebrow as she said, "Oh, I didn't think so. She suggested it because she could benefit from it."

Jimmy shook his head at Alice. "Why do you always have to question people's motives?"

Eddie removed his jacket from the back of his chair and slapped the dust off it. "Well, I've got to get to the drugstore. The boss doesn't like it when his part-timers come in late. He's a good guy and I don't like to take advantage of him."

He started toward the door, then stopped. Turning to Jimmy and Alice, he added, "Why don't the two of you sit down and try to figure out why this meeting failed? I think this project needs a faculty adviser as Charlie suggested. What's wrong with having someone around who's older and knows more? Maybe we're not as smart as we think we are. Ten students get together to work on a project in which they're all interested and—boom!—there's a clash of personalities. Well, maybe we should all go to the guidance office and find out why we couldn't get along with one another."

"There's a lot to what you say," agreed Jimmy. "Maybe we could all use some counseling."

Alice had been chewing on the eraser end of a long pencil, listening attentively to Eddie. Casually, Eddie brushed the pencil out of her mouth, said, "That's dirty," and then turned to Jimmy, and said, "Well, you two talk it over. I'm off to work."

Jimmy quickly grasped Eddie's jacket. "Hold it a minute. If we call another meeting next week, will you come?"

"Yes, I think so." Turning to Alice, Eddie said, "Be seeing you," and left the room.

*Ten young people had gathered in a room. Now there were two.*

Alice and Jimmy seated themselves at the front of the room. They were both frustrated and fatigued. Alice tilted her head and scratched her forehead slowly with her right forefinger, as

Jimmy threw his head back and stared at one of the lights on the ceiling.

"Jimmy," Alice said in a voice barely above a whisper.

Deep in thought, Jimmy continued to stare at the ceiling as he replied in a similarly quiet voice, "Yes?"

"I shouldn't be your assistant. It's silly. I can't do the things they expect of me. Maybe I'm a follower, not a leader. It was my fault. I should have made Billy feel welcome. But I couldn't. I think I needed someone to make me feel welcome. I don't know. Maybe I just haven't any personality."

Jimmy lowered his head and rubbed his eyes. The ceiling light was strong and his eyes had begun to smart. He arose and Alice did likewise. "Boy, that's funny. Nancy does everything wrong and blames everybody else. You didn't do anything wrong and you say it's your fault. Maybe it was my fault. Maybe all of us are at fault. Maybe none of us has any personality. Or, maybe something's wrong with the personalities we have. Maybe—maybe—maybe. Who knows?"

He stepped over to the front desk and gathered up his books. "How about having some ice cream before you go home?" he asked.

There was no hesitancy as Alice nodded her head affirmatively.

"Good. Let's go to the drugstore and get some sodas. I need some calories," he said.

*Ten young people had gathered in a room. Now there was one.*

Jimmy hastily pulled the sweater over his head, quickly adjusted the pullover and rejoined Alice. Before closing the door, he gazed around the empty room for a moment and then turned to Alice. "What went wrong?" he asked.

Alice was a picture of puzzlement. "I don't know. The only thing I do know is that everyone was so sensitive, so tender-skinned." After a moment's thought, she added, "Maybe that's what we should call ourselves, the 'Tender Ten.'"

Slowly closing the door behind him, Jimmy mused, "The 'Tender Ten.' That's a very good name for this group. I like it.

Now, let's go and see if we can figure out what happened to the 'Tender Ten,' " he said as they hurried down the hallway and out of the school building.

*Ten young people had gathered in a room. Now there were none.*

## WHAT WENT WRONG? WHAT HAPPENED?

In many ways, what happened in that room unfortunately happens so many times each day in so many different places.

Families sit down for dinner and one member says or does something which irritates another, and thus unhappily ends what might have been a pleasant evening. A parent and a child try to discuss a problem amicably and one or the other allows his temper to flare; so there is no discussion and no communication between the two. A fraternal organization holds a special meeting and one person insists on having his say and his way and continues to hold the floor until gradually the others leave the assembly hall; and thus nothing is accomplished.

Wherever and whenever several people meet, conflict may arise because one cannot control his anger, one is domineering, one is always belittling, one is overcome with jealousy, one is a bully, one is a snob, one is extremely sensitive, one is a braggart, one must always have things as he wants them, one derives peculiar pleasure out of saying something which will hurt another, and one after another behaves in such manner as to produce discord rather than harmony.

What is behind all of these conflicts? Eddie spoke of "a clash of personalities." Alice said, "Maybe I just haven't any personality." And Jimmy said, "Maybe there's something wrong with the personalities we have."

In one respect Eddie and Alice and Jimmy were correct—namely, in pinpointing "personality" as the root of their difficulties. Personality is an often misused and misunderstood term. Many people, including Alice, apply it only to those who are outgoing, aggressive and scintillating. Thus, they say that Peter, who is the captain of the debating squad, has "personality" and that Cynthia, who is the star of the school's annual dramatic show, also has "personality."

Well, this is true. Peter and Cynthia do have personality. But so too does Alice. And so too do Jimmy and Eddie and Dolores and Charlie and Susie—and YOU—and everyone else. Everybody has personality.

What is this "personality" which everyone has?

# 2
# PERSONALITY—WHAT IS IT?

IN ANCIENT TIMES, ACTORS IN THE GREEK THEATRES wore masks to identify the roles they were playing. *Persona* is Greek for "mask," and the masks indicated the specific part or "personality" of each actor.

Thus came the modern word "personality." Even now, you may hear someone refer to a person whom he does not especially like as one who "puts on an act." It is true that some people try to "mask" their true feelings by the "act" which they "put on." However, today personality is not viewed in this limited manner. Instead, it has a much broader, all-encompassing meaning.

*Your personality* is *your total behavior* in response to *your total environment.* Your personality differentiates you from your relatives, your friends and all other people. Each person's personality is different and distinct.

*Your* personality is all that *you* think and feel and say and do to *yourself* and to those with whom *you* come in contact during the course of *your* daily activities. Add up all *your* traits, *your* thoughts, *your* feelings, *your* attitudes, *your* wishes, *your* habits, *your* abilities, *your* interests and all the ways *you* act and react to *your* environment, and you will start to get some idea of the vast and complex nature of *your* personality.

## PERSONALITY TRAITS—POSITIVE AND NEGATIVE

Each person's personality includes specific, individual personal characteristics, known as personality traits. Some people are generally agreeable, pleasant and friendly; others are more often quarrelsome, grumpy and "carry a chip" on their shoulder. Some usually are cooperative and ready to be of assistance to their friends and relatives; others are self-centered and take a "what's in it for me" attitude. Some have admirable ambitions and aspirations; others drift drearily along from day to day.

Some people are exuberant and enthusiastic and have a zest for life; others are dull, dismal and dispirited. Some are typically optimistic and cheerful; others are pessimistic and gloomy. Some are loyal and honorably guard the confidences of others; some have no sense of loyalty and betray confidences unhesitatingly. Some are domineering; others are submissive. Some are hopeful; others are despairing. Some are aggressive; others are shy. Thus it goes with trait after trait.

We all have positive and negative personality traits. However, there are times when we exhibit traits, either positive or negative, which are not characteristic of our usual pattern of behavior. Thus, considerate people may sometimes be thoughtless; self-reliant people may have their episodes of dependency; tactful people have at times been tactless; timid people may act aggressive under certain unusual circumstances, and so on and on with each different characteristic.

We attribute a particular trait to a person when that quality describes his *typical* pattern of behavior. Compassionate people may have moments of heedlessness, but if they are usually thoughtful and sympathetic, we may aptly classify them as the latter.

## TRAITS OF THE TENDER TEN

There are a great many different personality traits. The Tender Ten displayed specific traits during their ill-fated meeting. However, each has far more traits—positive and negative—than those which he (or she) exhibited during that limited period of time.

*Billy* revealed the trait of shyness. He waited for his classmates to be friendly to him, and when they were not, he left. He should have taken the initiative and shown an interest in them and in their mutual project. He should have made efforts to be friendly toward them by sitting up front with the rest of the group, instead of staying in the back where he was unnoticed. Surely, then, some of the members of the group would have reciprocated in kind toward Billy. If you want others to be friendly toward you, you must be friendly toward them.

*Cathy* is overly sensitive. She must learn how to control her sensitivities, for she cannot control what others will say to her. There are several ways in which she might have responded to Frankie's abusiveness, other than by leaving the room as she did. She might have done any of the following: (1) counteracted Frankie's remark by topping it with a jibe aimed at Frankie, but this would have increased the hostilities; (2) ignored the remark; (3) laughed at it; or (4) agreed with Frankie that she is too obese. The latter three reactions would have disarmed him completely. The insulter's objective is to hurt his victim. If Cathy had ignored Frankie, laughed at his remark or agreed with him, she would have given him the impression that he had not hurt her. (Since Cathy does suffer from obesity, she should consult her family physician and school counselor, who in cooperation with each other could help her to understand why she is obese and how to correct the condition.)

*Frankie* is thoughtless and unkind. He is a bully; a bully is a frightened child who tries to cover up his fears by frightening and hurting others. He believes he has been rejected at home and feels hurt. He strikes out at others in a vain attempt to prevent further hurt to himself. Frankie is insecure in his estimate of himself as a young man. Participation in manly pursuits, such as athletic activities, would help to build his self-confidence and reduce his self-doubts. He must learn that his constant insults and lack of consideration make others uncomfortable in his presence. With the proper guidance, he could be helped to overcome his feelings of inadequacy and be able to accentuate his acceptable traits (and he does have these too!). He would then not need to insult Cathy (or anyone else) nor bully Nancy, and could become a more pleasant, positive group member.

*Nancy* is a faultfinder. She is displeased with herself and is plagued by feelings of inferiority. People who are not satisfied with themselves often find fault with others. In this way they aim to elevate themselves by reducing the stature of other people; however, their behavior accomplishes neither aim. On the contrary, their constant faultfinding emphasizes their own inadequacies and further reduces their own, already diminished stature. Nancy's evaluation of herself is so low that she feels unworthy of much. She, therefore, is submissive to Frankie in spite of his being cruel and coarse to her. Nancy should learn to look for the good qualities in others; this will make her more likable. She should also develop the positive resources which she possesses, and this would help to bring her some of the acceptance she craves.

*Susie* is a spoiled child. She is an only child and has been pampered a great deal by her parents. She must learn to accept the fact that she is not an "only child" to Jimmy or Alice or anyone else. She cannot and will not always have her way outside her home. Unless she accepts this fact, she will meet with frequent frustration and unhappiness. Susie's preoccupation with herself makes her very unattractive to her classmates. She must learn the importance of cooperation and that there is pleasure to be derived from being interested in others and from working together with others as a cooperative member of a group.

*Charlie* is thoughtful and considerate of the feelings of others. With sympathy for Cathy and anger at Frankie, he responded immediately to Frankie's insulting behavior toward Cathy. Satisfied with his achievements on the football field, he feels adequate as a young man and does not need to resort to artificial props, such as cigarettes, as Frankie does. Frankie considers Charlie domineering and a braggart (both of which are not so) because he envies Charlie's athletic prowess. Since Charlie has self-respect, he is able to give respect to those who deserve it. Thus, he welcomes the assistance of a faculty adviser, someone older and more knowledgeable, to guide them with their project.

*Dolores* is a pessimist. A member of a large family, she has seen a number of things go wrong for her parents and sisters and brothers. She has developed the habit of daydreaming, for in the world of unreality she makes everything turn out just right. Dolores should take the time to make an honest appraisal of her real world. She would find that there are many things right in it. A certain amount of daydreaming is normal and healthy, but like many other activities, when done to excess it can be quite harmful; excessive daydreaming removes the daydreamer too often from the real world to which he must adjust himself. Dolores should more actively immerse herself in school extracurricular activities where the contagious enthusiasm of bright young people will help bring her out of her pessimistic lethargy. She should engage in those activities in which she has competence, and her success in these will help her to develop more self-assurance.

*Eddie* should have extended a welcome to Billy, since he saw him enter. It was unfriendly of him not to have done so. It is incumbent upon each member of a group to extend a hand of friendship to other members. Eddie is a perfectionist and demands too much of himself and others. He should not expect this project to be "perfect," for the Tender Ten are high school students and not professionals. Cleanliness is a virtue, but extreme impeccability, such as Eddie's, often indicates an inner feeling of uncleanliness which the extraordinarily immaculate person attempts to conceal in this fashion. Eddie's holding a job after school hours is a wholesome effort on his part to build his self-esteem, but he should consult his school counselor to help him cope more adequately with his problem, whatever it may be.

*Alice* does not trust people. She has little confidence in herself and, therefore, is rather reticent. Some of her classmates have accused her of being a snob. The snob tries to give the appearance of being "above the crowd" because inwardly he feels "below the crowd." Jimmy has stated that she always questions people's motives, and this distrust of others indicates the presence of a personal problem for which she should seek help from her school counselor. With the proper guidance, she could build her self-confidence, become more secure and be capable of assisting Jimmy with this project.

*Jimmy* is a very bright young fellow, but he lacks leadership qualities. A good leader must be persuasive and have the ability to make people feel important so they will do happily what they might otherwise not like to do at all. He should have an enthusiastic optimism which would inspire the other members of the group. Jimmy must learn to treat group members with dignity and to make them feel they are partners in the project. As chairman, he should lead and give direction to the group and not be solely a listener. To insure success for the project, he should seek advice from the school counselor and obtain a faculty adviser as Charlie and Eddie suggested.

## YOUR TRAITS ON TRIAL

As you view the Tender Ten, there are some things about each one which you may like and some which you may dislike. What about yourself? What about *your* traits? Are you pleased with most of your personality traits, or are you displeased with many of them? Let's see if you can view yourself objectively. This is not easy to do, but you can try.

Take a piece of paper and draw a line down the center. At the top of the left-hand side write "What I Like about Myself," and at the top of the right-hand side write "What I Dislike about Myself." All right now, what do YOU like about YOU? What do YOU dislike about YOU? Try not to judge yourself too harshly, nor too easily either.

Do you get along well with the members of your family? Do you generally accept your share of responsibility at home, or are you more apt to shirk your duties? Are you ready to help when your assistance is requested at school? Do you lose your temper when you cannot have your way? Can you be relied upon to carry out a task assigned to you? Are you considerate of the rights of others? Are you prompt for your appointments?

Do you stop to think before you speak, or do you often say things which are offensive to others? Are you loyal to your relatives and friends? Do you have a cheerful disposition? Are you easily discouraged? Do you make friends readily? Are you often jealous of others? Do you seek out the positive qualities of people and admire them for them, or are you generally critical of those you know?

Consider the way you behave in your home, school and social settings and continue listing those characteristics which please you and those which displease you. As your list lengthens, you will find that you have many positive traits and a number of negative ones too (everyone has them). Carefully go down that list of what YOU like about YOU, and then do the same with the list of what YOU dislike about YOU. Place your traits on trial.

Now, look at those positive traits on your list. Have you brought these traits out into public view? If you are basically a generous person, did you join the teen division of your community drive or similar group and do your share? Have you shown how dependable and thoughtful you are by volunteering to do what you can at the local hospital? Unless you put your positive traits to use, they are not truly characteristic of you—so, use them and use them often.

What about the things you dislike about yourself? Are you making efforts to control and minimize them? Perhaps you would like to make some changes in your personality traits. You can change your behavior if you really want to. You can make changes that will increase your list of positive traits and decrease your list of negative traits.

## YOU CAN CHANGE

People who do not wish to change their ways try to defend their position by maintaining that people cannot change. This is not so. People can change. You can make changes for the better and improve your personality, if you have the determination to change.

Yes, YOU can change too. Your personality has tremendous potentialities for growth, for development, for change. This ability to change makes it possible for each of us to reduce the intensity of our undesirable negative traits and even ultimately to eliminate them completely. It also enables us to develop additional desirable positive traits and to strengthen those positive traits which we already possess. With the exception of some who are mentally ill, people can change if they have the sincere desire, if they have the will to do so.

However, although we can change our own personalities, we cannot change the behavior patterns of others (notwithstanding the fact that we at times attempt to influence others to make certain changes in themselves). Thus, if you are in a group situation and want to accomplish something for the mutual good of all concerned, you should put forth the effort to cooperate and meet the group members halfway, or more if necessary. Each member of a group should extend himself toward being a cohesive rather than a disruptive influence.

As you grow older and, hopefully, become more mature, you come face to face with new situations. Your maturity is gauged by your ability to adjust to these situations, and this adjustment generally requires changes within you. Thus, not only can you change, you often must change.

We are living in a time of tension, often called an age of anxiety. Down through the ages, people have lived with pressures. Today, however, the pressures on people are greater and more potent because of more problems. You must contend with the pressures of your home, your school, your friends and class-mates, your employer (if you work after school hours or during the summer months) and all the circumscribed society in the world in which you live. Your parents face your pressures—for your problems are their problems too—plus added ones of their own, of family and friends, of hearth and health, of employer and earnings and of present and future security.

Although some people (especially those who are immature) do not like to accept this fact, it is a fact nonetheless that problems are part of our existence. No one lives so charmed a life as to be without them. The vital task is to learn how realistically to con-front, cope with and conquer each problem as it presents itself. This must be done by consciously and wholesomely accepting your responsibilities and attacking your problems, and not by evading them or by attempting to shift the blame for them onto some innocent relatives, friends or acquaintances who just hap-pen to be within your range. By doing the latter, you will not be solving your immediate problem, and you will alienate your vic-tims. You will still have your original problem plus the added problem of your diminished personal popularity.

Unfortunately, millions of dollars are spent annually for head-ache pills and tranquilizers. Into the mouths of millions go multi-millions of palliative powders, pills, capsules and tablets aimed at helping mid-twentieth-century man to tolerate the tensions of our troubled times.

There are times when an aspirin or similar medication is neces-sary, but excessive need for and use of these palliatives could be stopped if people would face their problems consciously and cope with them on a realistic, rational basis. (Conscious approaches to problems are discussed in detail in Chapter 8.) Facing up to prob-lems often calls for changes in our attitudes, our feelings, our thoughts, our actions, and even sometimes in certain basic pat-terns of our behavior.

Often, the changes necessary are rather minor, and we are able to make them without assistance. Other times, however, the nature and intensity of the problems are such that more major changes are necessary and professional help is required.

## PEOPLE WHO CAN HELP

When you have a problem discuss it with your parents. It may be advisable too at times to seek the assistance of your family physician or your clergyman. There are additional people who are professionally trained and skilled to aid those who have problems. You, who are in school, have available to you the services of the school counselor (known too as the guidance counselor).

Your school counselor has had graduate-level training (beyond the college degree) in guidance and psychology and is equipped to aid you with your educational, personal, social and vocational problems. Feel free to consult your school counselor and discuss your problems with him. Whatever you tell him, he will not violate your confidence. The counselor does not tell you what to do; he does not come to any decisions for you. He helps you to get a better understanding of yourself, of your problems and of the world about you and thereby enables you to come to your own best possible decision. He thus helps you to help yourself.

Some schools also have on their staffs school psychologists. Counselors and psychologists are educated in the field of psychology, the science of human behavior. In the same school, the counselor and the psychologist generally work together to be of maximum assistance to their students. The counselor offers guidance on term programs, educational planning, future careers, college admissions and a variety of other personal problems of an educational, vocational and social nature; he administers group tests and conducts counseling sessions. The psychologist specializes in psychological testing and generally gives such tests to individual students as required.

Those who are not in school and do not have the services of a school counselor or school psychologist available to them should be especially careful in seeking assistance with their problems. Unfortunately, there are all too many untrained, unqualified persons in some localities who call themselves "counselors" and "psychologists" but are neither. When you need assistance, be sure you go to an approved counseling agency or to a qualified, registered psychologist. Competent professional assistance may also be available to you at the advisement, counseling or testing center at your local college or university.

For the names and addresses of approved counseling agencies, ask your school librarian or the librarian at your public library for a copy of the latest *Directory of Approved Counseling Agencies*, or send two dollars for a copy to the American Personnel and Guidance Association, 1605 New Hampshire Ave. N. W., Washington, D. C. 20009.

To check the qualifications of a psychologist you may wish to consult, write to your State Department of Education to determine whether he has been certified (if your state is one of those which registers psychologists who practice within that state), or write to the American Psychological Association, 1200 Seventeenth St. N. W., Washington, D. C. 20036, regarding his professional membership.

Beyond the confines of the school, there are a variety of psychologists. Thus, for example, there are the counseling psychologists who, in the main, work with normal people and help them to arrive at satisfactory adjustments to their problems; the clinical psychologists who serve in mental hospitals and clinics and administer specialized tests to the patients there; the industrial psychologists who apply psychological techniques to the selection and training of employees in industry; and the social psychologists who analyze the social forces which affect the behavior of human beings.

The psychiatrist, in contrast to the psychologist, is a physician who has completed postgraduate training in the medical specialty of psychiatry. Psychiatry is the science of mental and emotional disorders, and the psychiatrist is concerned with the diagnosis, prevention and treatment of these illnesses. Psychiatrists use varied forms of treatment, such as drug therapy, shock therapy and psychoanalysis; the latter is used too by some psychologists. Psychoanalysis is a procedure generally consisting of many sessions during which the analyst encourages the analysand (the person who is undergoing psychoanalytic treatment) to speak freely about his dreams, his thoughts, his memories or anything else he wishes, in order to reduce or eliminate the conflicts which are disturbing him.

## WHY YOU BEHAVE AS YOU DO

Why did each of the Tender Ten behave as he (or she) did? Why do YOU behave as YOU do?

No doubt you have at times wondered why you, at a certain time in a certain place, acted the way you did. Perhaps you were rather annoyed with yourself on these occasions. Why didn't you speak up when you wanted to voice your views? Why had you not controlled your temper? Why did you antagonize your friend? Why? Why? Why? How often we question our own behavior and wonder why we acted the way we did.

The science of psychology explains a great deal about the nature of our behavior, but the answers to these why's are not simple, because our personalities are not simple. Your personality is the complex totality of all your individual personality traits, your attitudes, your habits, your physical characteristics, your thoughts, your emotions, your actions and reactions to everyone and everything in your environment. It is all that is inside of you in all of its relationships and responses to all that is outside of you; all of the latter have their effect on your personality.

The time of day, the day of the week, the weather on a particular day and the seasons of the year directly or indirectly influence your behavior. Some people, for example, are more alert in the morning hours, whereas others are more responsive later in the day. The reactions of some are quite different on a Monday, at the start of a school- or work-week, than on a Friday, at the end of the week. A sunny day tends to make most of us more cheerful, whereas a rainy day is apt to bring on the feeling of gloom. Some people prefer cold weather; others prefer the warmth; and all react according to their seasonal preferences.

Within you, you are all with which you were endowed by nature, your heredity, plus all that your environment has done to maintain, to improve upon and/or to detract from it. Thus, you are the combined result of nature and nurture acting upon each other, sometimes in conflict and more often, hopefully, in cooperation.

Our behavior depends upon the many vital functions our bodies must perform. The human body has several specialized systems, each geared to perform some important function (or functions). The circulatory system, which includes the heart, blood and blood vessels, distributes nourishment throughout the body. The digestive system receives the food we consume, digests it, absorbs it and eliminates the remaining waste materials. The nervous system includes the brain, spinal cord and all of the nerves, which together permit us to respond to our environment and to function on the highest level of animal intelligence. The reproductive system consists of the sex organs, which make human reproduction possible.

Through the respiratory system, we breathe, supply oxygen to the body and remove carbon dioxide. The skeletal system, our bone structure, and the muscular system, which consists of all of the muscles, together support and protect us and enable us to move about; the skin, our protective covering and a vital sensory organ, plays an especially important role in our daily social life. The urinary system, with its kidneys, ureters, bladder and urethra, removes waste products which accumulate as a result of the activities of the billions of cells in the body.

Each of these systems is composed of special organs and tissues which, in turn, are made up of specialized cells, each so constructed as to best perform the functions of each respective system. These systems plus our several glands working together enable us to make the best possible adjustment to our environment. All of these systems, organs and glands, although each has its unique functions, are interrelated and interconnected. If any gland or any organ of any of the systems is ailing or injured, your behavior—your thoughts, your reasoning ability, your memory, your emotions, your attitudes, your actions and your reactions— may be immediately affected.

Remember that tummy ache you had after eating too many banana splits, or was it too many hamburgers? You weren't your typically pleasant self, were you? When you have a cold or a headache or a muscle spasm or any other malfunction, you don't behave as you normally would, do you? Similarly, your feelings and thoughts and attitudes affect your body systems and their functioning. Eating when one is angry and distressed, for example, may bring on a case of indigestion.

During the teen years, rapid body growth takes place, and a great many internal changes occur. Physiological (functional) changes do not happen at the same age for each young person, but when they do occur, they bring certain behavioral changes with them. Thus, for some girls, the onset of menstruation may occur as early as age nine or ten, whereas for others it may not come until they are as old as sixteen; for most girls, the onset occurs somewhere during the ages of twelve to fourteen. Similarly, the onset of puberty for boys is generally between the ages of thirteen and fourteen, but it may come as early as twelve for some boys and as late as seventeen for others.

Young people are often somewhat less concerned about their general health and fitness than they are about their appearance and popularity. However, the latter depend to a great extent upon your state of health and general body condition. If you want to make a better appearance, to increase your positive popularity and to improve your personality, physical fitness is a first must.

Physical fitness is an essential foundation for a wholesome, healthy personality. Good health is more than merely the absence of illness. It is also the active presence of vigor and vitality, of enthusiasm and energy, of a zest for living and a love of life. Your mental health and your physical health are interrelated and interdependent.

To maintain good health, you need proper food, sufficient sleep, adequate exercise, wholesome forms of relaxation and regular health check-ups, including medical, dental, eye, ear and foot examinations. Every young person should have a suitable, well-balanced breakfast before leaving for school in the morning. Personal habits of cleanliness and good grooming should accompany physical fitness. Your morale will be higher, and your appearance and behavior will reflect this, if you are and look neat and clean and if you dress tastefully and appropriately.

For an authoritative complete home program for physical fitness, girls should get a copy of *Vim: A Complete Exercise Plan for Girls 12 to 18* and boys a copy of *Vigor: A Complete Exercise Plan for Boys 12 to 18*. Both of these pamphlets were prepared by the President's Council on Physical Fitness, and they may be obtained by sending twenty-five cents for each to the Superintendent of Documents, United States Government Printing Office, Washington, D. C. 20402.

## THE A-B-C OF YOUR PERSONALITY

You have just learned that you behave the way you do because of the relationships and responses of all that is inside of you with and to all that is outside of you. On this basis, it can be said that your personality has anthropological, biological and cultural (environmental) foundations.

From the interactions of these three foundations, there subsequently emerge the intellectual, emotional and mental aspects of your personality. Although one or more of these may assume greater dominance and play a more prominent role in your present personality, they are all closely interconnected and inseparable. We will examine them separately as we go along in order to give you a clearer understanding of these influences, to help you to know more about why you act as you do, and to indicate the vast potentiality of your personality.

Anthropologically, your personality has its origins in periods centuries before you were born. This may sound strange to you at first. But think a moment. It is this very thinking which distinguishes you and all other human beings from most other members of the animal kingdom. As a member of the species *Homo sapiens* you stand at the apex of the evolutionary process as the most intelligent of all animals. There are some animals that have the capacity to think and some that are able to voice sounds, but only human beings have the capacity to think creatively, to assimilate information, to remember, to express their thoughts and information in speech, to reason and thereby improve upon their accumulated knowledge, and to transmit this knowledge to their fellow human beings.

These uniquely human capabilities are the result of our well-developed nervous system. It is the human nervous system, with its highly complex brain and spinal cord, which qualifies us to think, to reason, to solve problems and consequently to make the highest level of adjustment to our environment.

Even the lowest forms of animal life have some capacity to react to the outside world. Thus, the amoeba, the simplest form of animal life, a protozoan consisting of merely one single cell, is capable of withdrawing from an unfavorable environment because its cellular protoplasm possesses the power of irritability. This, however, is not an intelligent response to its environment, since no thought processes are involved.

The hydra, a simple coelenterate, a somewhat higher form of life, has a primitive nervous system consisting of nerve fibers and nerve cells. In the earthworm, a slightly more complex metazoan, there are a nerve cord and a very primitive brain. As we continue along up the rungs of the animal kingdom, we come to the frog and the fish, which possess nervous systems composed of the two essentials, the brain and the spinal cord. Their brains, however, are very tiny and poorly developed.

Many anthropological and biological changes took place before the brain arrived at its most highly developed state in species *Homo sapiens.* How did it get that way? What does it consist of (its anatomy)? How does it function (its physiology)? To find the answers to these questions, let us look in on your V.I.B., that *Very Important Brain* of yours.

# 3

# YOUR V. I. B.

## (VERY IMPORTANT BRAIN)

THE CENTRAL NERVOUS SYSTEM, CONSISTING OF THE
brain and the spinal cord, is one of the most complex systems
within the human body. It is this system which makes it possible
for us to appreciate and understand the world in which we live.
It enables us to act and react, to think and reason, to sense and
feel. It qualifies us to speak, to see, to hear, to smell, to touch, to
walk, to laugh, to cry and to respond and communicate in a vast
variety of ways with the world around us.

Often, the human nervous system is compared to a telephone
switchboard with its incoming and outgoing calls and many
possible connections. Telephone wires are bound together to
form cables, and nerve fibers are bound to form nerves; cables
and nerves carry messages in the form of electrical energy. However, the human central nervous system can do what the telephone system cannot. It is capable of storing facts, of remembering, of generating thoughts and of carrying out intricate mental
activities as a result of the unique nature of nerve tissue.

The nervous system is one of the first systems of the body
to start and the last to complete its development. When a female
germ cell (ovum) and a male germ cell (sperm) unite, an

40

embryo is formed. The nerve tissue of the human being is derived from the ectoderm, the outer layer of the embryo.

## THE DEVELOPMENT OF THE BRAIN

The ectoderm forms a thick band, called the neural plate, along the midline of the embryo. The center of this plate becomes depressed, giving rise to the neural groove, which is bounded by two elevations, the neural folds. This groove appears before the embryo is three weeks old. Not long thereafter, the neural groove becomes deeper, the neural folds approach each other and fuse, and the neural tube is formed.

As early as the fourth week of life, when the embryo is only about 2.5 mm. in length, the anterior end of this neural tube constricts to form the three primary vesicles of the human brain—namely, the prosencephalon, the mesencephalon and the rhombencephalon. The posterior portion of the neural tube eventually forms the spinal cord.

During the ensuing months, the prosencephalon (forebrain), the mesencephalon (midbrain) and the rhombencephalon (hindbrain) undergo tremendous change and growth. The forebrain becomes the large mass of gray and white tissue which fills the entire upper portion of the skull cavity and is known as the cerebrum; it is shaped like an egg and consists of two halves called cerebral hemispheres. The hindbrain develops further and divides into the cerebellum, the pons and the medulla oblongata. Thus, the human brain consists of five distinct but interrelated and connected parts: (1) the massive cerebrum, (2) the smaller midbrain, (3) the cerebellum, (4) the pons and (5) the medulla oblongata.

In about the sixth month of fetal life, a most important development takes place. If you have been to a butcher store or to the meat department in a supermarket recently, you probably have seen animal brains in the showcase or on the counter. Did you notice the surface of the brains and the furrows in the brain tissue? If you did not, make a note to look the next time you are in the store. When you do look, you will see that the brain surface has irregular folds and ridges.

Until about the sixth month, the surface of the embryonic human brain is smooth (lissencephalic). Thereafter, fissures and convolutions begin to appear rapidly. Fissures are indentations or furrows, and the convolutions are the ridges between these furrows. These develop because the gray matter starts to increase quickly by spreading out in a thin sheet rather than by increasing in thickness, thus causing the surface of the brain to become convoluted. This development is extremely important because studies have shown that the nature and degree of the convolutions of our brain are directly related to our intellectual capacities.

## WHY THE BRAIN IS SO "BRAINY"

The difference between man's mental ability and that of other members of the animal kingdom appears to be dependent upon the following two factors: (1) the great size of the human brain and (2) its many convolutions. However, neither factor alone is sufficient to explain the difference.

The average adult human male has a brain weight of approximately 1360 grams and the average adult human female approximately 1250 grams. The average brain weight of the elephant is 5430 grams. Thus, the elephant's absolute brain weight exceeds man's. However, whereas the average adult human male has a brain weight to body weight ratio of 1:42 (i.e., one pound of brain weight for each forty-two pounds of body weight) and the average adult human female a ratio of 1:40, the elephant's brain weight in comparison to his body weight shows a ratio of 1:500. Therefore, although the elephant is superior to man in absolute brain weight, he is far inferior to man in relative brain weight.

There are two small mammals, known as *Midas midas* and

*Ateles ater,* which have brain weight to body weight ratios of 1:26 and 1:15 respectively. However, the surfaces of the brains of these animals have very few convolutions and are almost entirely smooth. Then again, in regard to convolutions, we find that the mammals known as the *Proboscidia* and the *Cetacea* have the most highly convoluted brains, even more convoluted than the human brain; however, their brain weight is far inferior to man's.

If man does not rank first among the mammals in absolute brain weight, nor relative brain weight, nor the degree of convolutions, to what then can we attribute his superior intelligence? It is believed that man's greater intellectual capacities can be attributed to his possession of the best existing combination of brain weight and highly convoluted cerebral surface. It is this combination which has given to *Homo sapiens* his unique thinking and reasoning abilities. It is this combination which has made yours a very special, very important brain.

## THE ANATOMY OF THE BRAIN AND SPINAL CORD

The human brain is an extremely complex structure and the most amazingly coordinated mechanism. For a long time, physiologists believed that certain areas of the brain controlled specific body functions. It is only recently, however, that scientists have been able to localize some of these areas.

By experimenting with animals and by studying persons who had suffered brain injuries, scientists have found that there are special centers of the cerebrum controlling certain of our activities. Thus, there is a *motor area* which sends impulses to the muscles and thereby controls our movements; there is a *sensory area* which is involved with body sensations. Within these areas, there are smaller centers concerned particularly with one specific function. The sensory area, for example, includes a visual (sight) center, an auditory (hearing) center, a gustatory (taste) center, an olfactory (smell) center and other lesser sensory centers. In addition to the motor and sensory areas, there are *association areas* in the cerebrum which contain nerve fibers connecting the motor and sensory areas.

When a center in the cerebrum is disabled or destroyed by illness or accident, other cerebral areas often have been able, to a lesser or greater degree, to assume the work of the ill or injured center. It has not been possible as yet to localize a particular area as the center for creative thinking. There are many who believe that the entire cerebral cortex (outer surface of the cerebrum), rather than one local area, is involved in the very complex activities of learning and creativity.

Directly below the cerebrum is the midbrain, which was mentioned earlier in this chapter. This is a small mass of tissue which connects the cerebrum with the hindbrain and contains nerve fibers descending from the cerebrum and other nerve fibers ascending from the hindbrain and the spinal cord. The midbrain also has nerve centers important in motor coordination.

The hindbrain, with its cerebellum, pons and medulla oblongata, is located below the midbrain. The cerebellum is found in the lower, posterior portion of the skull cavity, and none of its functions are on the conscious level; it is involved in maintaining body balance and equilibrium, muscle tone and the coordination of our movements. The pons acts as a bridge connecting other divisions of the brain with each other and allowing for the passage of nerve fibers from and to these parts. The medulla oblongata is the bulbous portion of the hindbrain which is connected to the spinal cord; in addition to joining the brain with the spinal cord, the medulla contains nerve fibers which are concerned with the vital functions of the heart, lungs, stomach and other essential organs.

From the brain, there emerge twelve pairs of vital cranial nerves, some of which are motor nerves, some sensory nerves, and others that combine motor and sensory fibers and are called mixed nerves.

The spinal cord is housed in the spinal column, which is a connected series of individual bones called vertebrae. The spinal cord consists of five regions: cervical, thoracic, lumbar, sacral and coccygeal. A total of thirty-one pairs of spinal nerves emerge from these regions. The spinal cord serves too as a pathway for nerve impulses to and from the brain. It is also a center of reflex action for nerve impulses to and from all the regions of the spine out to the trunk and limbs of the body.

## THE NATURE OF NEURONS

The nerve tissue of the brain and spinal cord is composed of highly specialized cells, nerve cells, scientifically known as neurons. Neurons are unlike other human cells in that they have long fibers, sometimes two or three feet in length, extending from one end of the cell body. These fibers are known as axons, and at their ends are very fine terminal branches. At the opposite end of the cell body of each neuron are short, thick branches called dendrites.

The dendrites of one neuron interlace with the final terminal branches of the axon of another neuron to form a synapse. It is through such synapses that nerve impulses are transmitted from one nerve cell to another until the message which is being carried arrives at its destination.

The neurons and their fibers are capable of making vast numbers of connections within the brain and of interrelating and connecting the many different areas of the brain with each other and with the spinal cord and other parts of the body. There are billions—yes, billions—of these nerve cells, and an almost unimaginable number of synaptic connections can be made among them. These connections represent potentials—potentials to adjust, to learn, to remember, to reason, to think, to solve problems, to create.

We can all perform on a higher level than that on which we are performing. We can all do better than we are doing, for so many billions of these possible connections are not used and represent wasted potentials.

Neurons have two special characteristics—namely, their power to react to stimulation (this is known as irritability or excitability) and their power to carry these stimuli or "messages" to other cells (this is known as conductivity or the ability to transmit nerve impulses).

There are three basic types of neurons: sensory, association and motor. Sensory fibers are so called because they receive their messages from sense organs, such as the eyes, ears, nose, tactile centers in the skin, and other centers of sensation. Because they receive the stimuli for transmittal to the brain, they are also known as receptor fibers. Since the motor fiber transmits the nerve impulse from the brain to the organ which effects a response to the stimulus, it is also known as an effector fiber.

The sensory neuron receives the stimulus (that force, thing or being which activates something else) and converts it into a nerve impulse. The nerve impulse is a burst of electrical energy, and this "electricity" is carried along the nerve fiber to the brain. There, the nerve impulse is transmitted to an association neuron which connects one region of the brain with another. This nerve fiber carries the impulse to a motor neuron whose fiber, in turn, is in contact with a muscle or gland. The latter receives the impulse, and then responds to the original stimulus.

Thus, for example, you are standing on a street corner waiting for the traffic light to change. Your eyes see the "WALK" lights go on. The sensory fibers carry this message from the eyes to the brain, where the nerve impulse is then transmitted by association fibers to motor fibers which, in turn, carry the impulse to the muscles of your legs, and you then begin to walk across the street. All of this happens so quickly that you are unaware of all the internal activity which enabled you to respond to the stimulus, in this case, the change in the traffic light. You are, however, aware of the traffic sign, of your desire to cross the street and of your actual crossing.

Many of our daily activities do not include awareness or thinking, and the cerebral neurons are not involved. These acts can be performed without the impulses traveling to the brain. Among these are the reflexes. A *reflex act* is a simple automatic response of a muscle or gland resulting from stimulation of a sense organ with which it is associated. Thus, you place your hand on the handle of a pot on the stove. The handle is very hot. The heat of the handle acts as a stimulus on the receptor neurons in your fingers and in the palm of your hand. Nerve impulses are generated and the sensory fibers transmit these impulses through the arm and into the spinal cord. Here the impulses pass across synapses formed by the sensory and association neurons and across other synapses formed by the association neurons and motor neurons, along the motor fibers and on to the appropriate arm and hand muscles, which promptly contract, resulting in the withdrawal of your hand from the handle of the pot. Thus, a simple reflex act occurred and the brain was not called into action.

Another form of automatic behavior is the habit. A *habit* is an act or process of behavior which has been repeated so often that it has become a part of you and requires little or no attention to its performance. If, for example, you have formed the habit of brushing your teeth each morning, you may do it so automatically that a little while after you have gone through the motions you may wonder whether you did or did not brush your teeth. Some habits are not fully automatic and involve certain active mental processes.

## MATTER—GRAY AND WHITE

When a parent or teacher or friend wants you to think of what you are doing, he may say, "Go ahead and use your gray matter."

Exactly what is "gray matter"? The gray matter is the combination of the synapses and the cell bodies of the neurons. The white matter consists of the long fibers. The fibers are grouped together to form nerves; thus, nerves are white in appearance.

The cortex, the outer surface of the cerebrum, is made up of layers of gray matter. Inside the cerebrum is white matter consisting of the nerve fibers which connect the different sections of the brain with each other and connect the brain with the spinal cord. In the spinal cord, the reverse is found; the outer layer is composed of white matter and the inner core of gray matter.

When someone speaks of "gray matter," he is referring essentially to the gray matter of the cerebral cortex. Since our thinking, reasoning, remembering and all our other high-level mental activities emanate from the cortex, the term "gray matter" has come to be associated with these activities. Similarly, someone may describe a friend as having "a brilliant mind" and continue on to say that he "uses his gray matter."

Just what is meant by the term "mind"? You have probably been told many times to "make up your mind." What is this mind that you have been asked to make up, and of what is it made up?

## THE MAKEUP OF YOUR MIND

Often, people use the terms "mind" and "brain" as though they were synonymous, which they are not.

The brain is tangible. It consists, as you have now learned, of masses of nerve tissue, the vast bulk of which is housed within the skull. The mind, however, is intangible. When you are told to "make up your mind," you are being directed to think, to decide, to come to some conclusion. All of the mental functions which constitute the mind flow forth from the cerebral cortex. Thus, the mind emanates from the brain.

The mind is made up of all of your mental processes—your thoughts, your reasoning, your imagination, your feelings, your attitudes, your memories, your dreams, your perceptions, your motivations and all of your other varied mental activities—and all of the controls which you consciously or unconsciously exercise over these mental processes.

All of the thought processes and other activities of the mind are a result of the synaptic connections of the neurons of the cerebral cortex. The highest level of mental activity is the process of *thinking*. Human beings are capable of magnificent artistic, literary, musical, scientific and other noteworthy accomplishments because of their thoughts and the *reasoning ability, imagination* and *creativity* which evolve from these thoughts. The ability to solve problems, to use one's imagination, to think and go forward from one piece of knowledge to another and another and another, and to progress thus to some splendid creative achievement is a unique capacity of the human mind.

Your *feelings* are your *emotions* and these are discussed in detail in Chapter 6. *Attitudes* are inclinations toward certain social and other values. Your attitudes are reflected in your behavior toward certain people, places and things. *Memory* is the ability to store and recall, in a manner ranging from vague to vivid, episodes which occurred in the immediate yesterday of the present or in the distant yesterdays of many years ago. The mind is capable of storing these experiences of the near and far-off past and then bringing them forth for recall. This storage and recall are essential for our complex thinking processes.

*Dreams* consist of fleeting or persistent images which appear while we are in a state of sleep. Psychologists and psychiatrists offer many explanations as to the nature and meanings of dreams, but dreams still offer luxuriant opportunities for further investigation. Dreams may portray things which we would like to have happen or things which we would not like to have happen and are afraid may happen; often, too, they represent unresolved conflicts, or they bring back past experiences which were repressed in our wakeful states.

The images which appear in our dreams may be clothed in symbols, and their actual meanings may be disguised; during psychoanalytic sessions, the analyst may probe into the hidden meanings of these symbols to help him determine what it is that may be disturbing the patient. Dreams are particularly fascinating to laymen and professionals alike because they give us clues to what is going on in the hidden inner recesses of our mind.

*Perception* is the recognition and interpretation of a sensory stimulus (or stimuli). Past experiences play important roles in perception; when something or someone stimulates our eyes or ears or nose or any of our other sense organs, we interpret this stimulus on the basis of our previous relationships with that stimulus. Thus, when you arrive at the corner of a street, the traffic light stimulates your eyes and, via these sense organs, you receive the *sensation* brought about by the red light. The mental processes involved in perception then enable you to interpret this sensation on the basis of your past association with it, and you know that you must stop and may not go again until the light turns green; a red light in a different setting may bring a similar sensation, but the perception of it would differ.

*Motivation* has a tremendous influence on your behavior, for it prods you on to a specific action. Your motivations are your drives; they are the urges which impel you to act. Some people have more motivation than others. There are those who, despite unfavorable circumstances, attended night school and did without necessities in order to obtain a good education; others, possibly in more favorable circumstances, may blame their inadequate education on lack of opportunity, when perhaps the basic cause was lack of sufficient motivation.

There are many psychologists and psychiatrists, especially those who are adherents of the late Dr. Sigmund Freud, who speak of the mind in terms of three major components: the *ego*, the *id* and the *superego*. The ego represents our conscious being and includes such mental activities as memory, perception and reasoning. The id is our unconscious being, enveloping our basic desires, drives and instincts (an *instinct* is a response or type of behavior which appears to be inborn rather than acquired, such as self-preservation); the unconscious includes the factors which act upon us and of which we are unaware. The superego is the controlling force which acts as the authority over the ego and the id; it forms the conscience and represents that area of our personality which encompasses our standards and ethics.

The more you use your mind, the more it will develop and flourish. Think! Put your mind to work. The more you exercise mentally, the better for you. Participate in games which stimulate you to think. Do crossword and other similar puzzles. Play checkers and chess. Solve problems. Read good books, magazines and newspapers. Stay mentally alert; keep your mind active and life will be far more meaningful, more exciting, more challenging for you.

## YOUR V.I.B. SPECIFICALLY

We are all fortunate indeed to be the possessors of this most remarkable, most intricate of all mechanisms, the human brain—this most fantastic machine which enables us to respond to several stimuli at one time and to one stimulus in several ways at the same time. This is indeed an extraordinarily constructed apparatus, which enables human beings to reach the acme of creativity.

This then is the human brain. But what about your individual human brain, YOUR V.I.B. specifically?

YOU are the sum total of all of the forces and factors resulting from your anthropological origins, your membership in the human race and your genetic inheritance from your parents, grandparents, great-grandparents and all your earlier forebears (popularly known, in its totality, as *nature*), and all of the factors and forces influencing you in all of the environments in which you have lived and are now living (popularly known, in its totality, as *nurture*). Thus, YOU specifically are the product of YOUR nature and YOUR nurture.

For many long years, controversies have raged on the ques-

tion of heredity versus environment and which of these factors
has greater importance in determining the future course of your
development. Some psychiatrists, psychologists and other behavioral scientists have given greater weight to hereditary influences; others, among these same groups of scientists, have
expressed strong sentiments in favor of environmental influences.
Today, the pendulum of scientific opinion has swung toward
greater emphasis on the powerful influences of our environment.

Your brain specifically provides you with tremendous potential for positive accomplishments. Your inherited genes offer you
a vast scope of possibilities and capabilities. Your genes also
present certain delimiting influences, but there is generally a
vast range of potentials even within these delimitations. There are
billions of potential brain cell connections, synaptic contacts,
which make it possible for you to function on a higher level. You
are capable of doing better than you are doing.

None of us ever achieves all that it is possible for us to
achieve. Unfortunately, our potentials remain in great part un-
fulfilled throughout our lifetime. It is nurture which must provide
the fertile fields, the soil and stimulus, in which the potentials
of nature may unfold and come to as full fruition as possible.

# 4
# RELATIVE TO YOUR RELATIONS

YOUR ENVIRONMENT HAS ENORMOUS EFFECT ON THE growth and development of your budding personality. From the moment you were born, you became a member of a specific society, also known as your sociocultural setting.

Your parents, their circle of relatives and friends, the house in which you lived and the street and neighborhood in which it was located, and the mores of the specific city and state in which you were born, all played important roles in establishing certain patterns of your future behavior. The foundations of so many facets of your present behavior—such as the language you speak and the regional accent with which you speak it, your manner of dress, the way you walk, the kinds of food you prefer, the books you read, the music to which you listen, and your hopes and aspirations—were set many years back on the basis of your early sociocultural setting. Most important of all, in determining your future development, was your specifically delimited home environment.

Your parents and their relationships toward you from the time of your birth up through your childhood days set the patterns, positive and negative, for many of your present acts, ideas and ideals. In addition to your parents, in your early days, there may have been numerous other people—doctors, nurses, brothers,

53

sisters, grandparents and other relatives, friends of your parents, neighbors and a greater or lesser number of other people according to the position of your parents and the circles within which they traveled. As you grew older, you added your own friends and their parents to this number. Then came your teachers and classmates in nursery school, kindergarten, elementary school and up through your present grade.

Your relationships with all of these people—the examples they set for you to follow, their actions toward you and your reactions toward them—played relevant roles, some lesser, some greater, in influencing your future behavior. The most important of all of these people, the people who wielded the greatest influence on you, were and are your parents.

## PARENTS ARE PEOPLE

Yes, parents are people. Teen-agers sometimes have their days of doubt and wonder whether their parents came from some other planet. But parents are earthlings and so, like other humans, they have their virtues and their faults. People are imperfect and parents too have their imperfections. But despite these imperfections, they generally possess many excellent qualities, one of the most important being their intense interest in your welfare.

Mothers and fathers, like all other people, have their own distinct characteristics. Some are warm and tender to their children, whereas others, although they too love their children dearly, are cold and withdrawn. Your parents' total personality traits have great effect on your personality development.

Your father's occupation, your mother's occupation (if she is employed), the education and special training of your parents, their basic values and standards of behavior, their aspirations, their individual accomplishments, their participation and position in the community, their emotional expressions and feelings toward each other and toward others—all of these factors and

everything else about your parents are of importance in determining the kind of person you become.

"If this is so," many people often ask, "how come siblings
(brothers and sisters) are frequently so very different from one
another?"

Well, first, as I indicated in Chapter 3, every person—brothers
and sisters included—has his own inherited genetic patterns, and
each one is constitutionally different. Also, this dissimilarity between siblings is due to the fact that these brothers and sisters
*did not* have the *same* parents. Invariably, this statement evokes
a chorus of, "Oh, we're not speaking of stepbrothers or stepsisters. We're speaking of brothers and sisters who *did* have the
same parents."

I am not speaking of stepbrothers or stepsisters either. I am
speaking of siblings born to the same set of parents. These parents, however, were different people to each of their children.

## PARENTS ARE DIFFERENT PEOPLE

Let us, for example, consider Frankie's parents. When Frankie's
older sister was born, his mother and father were new at parent-
hood. They were ecstatic at the arrival of the baby. For two
years, the little girl held the special status of the first-born and
only child. The child was smotherd with solicitude, and her
every wish was granted. Frankie's father's earnings were adequate to meet the needs of the small family.

When Frankie arrived, the home environment he entered was
quite unlike that into which his older sister had been born. A
month before Frankie appeared, his father lost his job. He did
not find another suitable position until Frankie was almost three
months old. In the meantime, family expenses had risen beyond
the father's abilities to meet them. Frankie entered a very an-
guished world.

Frankie's older sister had had a calm, contented mother, a

woman who had been delighted with the arrival of her first off-spring. Frankie had a mother who was nervous and discontented. She was worried about the growing number of unpaid bills and was overcome by ambivalent feelings toward her son; she was pleased to have a son, yet she was displeased with the additional burdens, financial and otherwise, which he had brought with him.

What of Frankie's father? When his first child was born, he was a demonstrative, devoted, doting father to his daughter. He hurried home from work to spend as much time as possible playing with her. The loss of his job just prior to Frankie's birth made him irritable and the victim of periodic headaches. He might have enjoyed playing with Frankie, but the new job had longer hours and was not as satisfying as the one he had held previously. Thus, he had neither the time nor the inclination to romp with Frankie as he had with his daughter. The affection he had showered on his daughter turned into a tiny trickle toward his son.

Did Frankie and his older sister have the *same* parents? Not really. Circumstances change. People change. Personalities change. From the time of Frankie's sister's birth to the time of his arrival, circumstances had changed a great deal for Frankie's parents, and his parents' altered personalities reflected these changes.

When Frankie was two years old, his younger sister was born. His mother had been ill much of the time during this pregnancy. She had not really wanted a third child so soon. She had problems enough stretching her husband's salary to meet the expenses of a family of four and had become tense and troubled trying to determine how she would manage for five.

Frankie's father sought and found an additional part-time job for evening hours and Saturdays. He needed the extra income to supplement his regular paycheck, but he was also pleased to be away from home during these hours, for his headaches had become more frequent and he found it easier to be at work than to tolerate the screaming and shouting at home. Frankie's older sister had resented his entry into the family circle, for her parents had in no way prepared her for him. She often quarreled with him, with or without provocation. The hostility which the older sister directed toward him, Frankie in turn transferred onto his younger sister, whom he would strike in his state of anger. The intrafamily feuds and fights were frequent.

Alone at home, Frankie's mother became increasingly excitable and shouted at Frankie for his slightest indiscretion. Most of her attention she directed to the baby of the family. On Sundays, when the father was home, his fondness for his first-born was obvious to Frankie, who stood as a forlorn, forgotten figure between his older and younger sisters.

In their relationships with their children, some parents become wiser as they grow older and learn from their experiences; others, possibly owing to illness, financial reverses or other unfortunate circumstances, become less adequate and find greater difficulty coping with their problems and their children's problems.

Stop now and consider the personalities of Frankie's parents, his older sister's parents and his younger sister's parents. Consider the parents' characteristics, their attitudes, their displays of affection, their personal health, their feelings of security and insecurity, their respective enthusiasm and lack of it at the arrival of each child, and their individual actions and reactions to each. Viewed in this manner, you will find that you are examining three separate sets of parents. Each child at birth and at each step of individual development had distinctly different parents.

In considering Frankie and his sisters and his parents, remember that his is a specific case. People are specific, not general. Each person is unique in the way he behaves in relation to the circumstances and forces around him. Faced with the seemingly same circumstances, one person will react in one way and another will react in the very opposite way.

## OLDEST, YOUNGEST, IN-BETWEEN AND ONLY CHILD

The oldest member of a family is not always excessively pampered, nor is the youngest always overprotected as in Frankie's family; nor is the middle child always ignored as Frankie was. Susie is an only child and her parents have indulged her every wish; but not every only child is a spoiled child, nor is every spoiled child an only child. In each family, the relationships between the parents and their children are specific to that family.

Wherever YOU are in your family—oldest, youngest, in-between or only child—it is important for you to understand and appreciate that your parents in their relationships with you are attempting to act in a way which they think is best for you. You may not always agree with them. You are a distinctly unique individual and they too are distinct unique individuals. There is no reason why you should agree one hundred per cent of the time. But you should make every effort to understand and cooperate with them, to appreciate the fact that they are more knowledgeable than you are (although this is a fact which it is difficult for many young people to accept) and to give them their due respect.

Unfortunately for many young people—although they may not consider it unfortunate at the time it is taking place—there are those who have been very indulged ("spoiled") by their parents. The only child and the youngest child are often expected to be spoiled children. However, frequently this is not so. In a family of two or more children, any one of the children for a variety of reasons, regardless of his place in the family lineup, may have been indulged more than the others by the parents. Thus, any child—oldest, youngest, in-between or only child—may be a spoiled child.

### SPOILED BY EVERY THING

Spoiled children have received many, many things from their parents but have not been required to give anything in return.

These young people are unfortunate because they have been given a false view of the world. They have been led to believe that the world too will grant them their every wish because their parents have done so. The truth is that the world does not grant us everything we want. Another important truth is that many of the things we want in this world are frequently not good for us.

The spoiled child's parents uniformly say they have given their child "everything"; but they haven't. They have given their child "every thing." There is a great big difference between "every thing" and "everything." "Every thing" refers to every material *thing*, every tangible item given to the child. "Everything" would need to include a basic set of moral standards, a code of wholesome values and the motivation to adhere to the teachings of the Golden Rule—and few, if any, spoiled children have been given these.

Spoiled children often develop self-centered, unattractive personalities and invariably have more difficulty getting along in the world than do those who have been taught to have a sense of responsibility, to have self-respect and to show respect for the rights of others. When they go out into the world and do not get every specific thing they want, or a particular wish is not granted, a minor matter may become a major calamity, and the spoiled child is headed for trouble.

Stop a moment. Think of all the adults, male and female (other than your parents), whom you know—your grandparents, sisters, brothers, other relatives, school principal, teachers, counselor, coach, librarian, physician, dentist, pharmacist, mail carrier, grocer, butcher, tailor, supermarket salesclerk, and so on and on. Now, answer this question: How many of these men and women are your mother and father? No, this question is not meant to be facetious.

The answer is obviously, "None," and the question is meant to highlight the fact that a young person who has been coddled by his parents acts as though all of the adult males in this world are his father and all the adult females are his mother. Because he has become accustomed to bullying his parents and getting his way with them, he thinks he can do likewise with all other adults (and children too) in his environment.

If your parents have not insisted on propriety, it may come as a surprise to you to discover that the adults outside your home will insist upon it. The "spoiled brat" behavior which was tolerated (if not totally accepted) at home is neither accepted nor tolerated outside the home. If you are not cooperative and considerate at school, on the job and in the world at large, you will find yourself rejected by your elders and your peers.

If you are one of these unfortunate young people who have been spoiled and if you can face up to this fact honestly, you can save yourself the heartaches of an unhappy future face to face with frustration. You can help yourself by making immediate efforts to change your behavior and start to treat others as you want others to treat you. People can change. People do change.

If you wish to be accepted as a young adult, you must behave like an adult. If you want to be trusted by your parents, show them you can be trusted. Demonstrate self-respect and show respect for the rights of others. Accept your share of family chores. Stand on your own two feet. Carry your own weight and, where necessary, share in helping someone else carry his weight if, unfortunately, a disability makes him unable to do so himself.

## SIBLINGS AND QUIBBLINGS

Quibbling among siblings is a popular pastime during the pre-teen and teen years. This practice is so prevalent that it is probably absent only in the family where there is an only child. Rivalry among sisters and brothers is perfectly normal when they are young.

If you have brothers and/or sisters, you know that you have a fundamental feeling of love toward each other. Between some siblings, this feeling may be stronger or weaker than between others, but generally there is a basic bond of concern. If the boy who lives down the block or the girl who lives across the street does not behave properly, you may be little or not at all upset by it. If, however, it is your brother or your sister who has misbehaved, you become very much concerned. Because of this concern, battles and bickering often develop between brothers and sisters regarding the individual behavior of each.

Sometimes, the feeling of love between siblings can give way temporarily to feelings of envy, jealousy and even hate. Nancy has a younger brother, and there are times when she feels as though she despises him. When Nancy was born, her father hoped for a son. He never quite knew how to play with or act toward Nancy. A year and a half later, Nancy's brother was born. Their father found it much easier to get along with his son than with his daughter, although he loved Nancy no less than he did the boy. However, Nancy felt rejected and unloved, since her brother received all of her father's attention.

Nancy often resented her brother, and whenever something went wrong, she blamed him. She frequently fought with him and sometimes even hit him. When their father came to the boy's defense, this angered her all the more. It should have been demonstrated to her that her parents loved her as much as they loved her brother, and they should have explained that during the growing stages, boys are less mature than girls of the same age, and since her brother was younger than she, he required more attention than she did. There would have been less likelihood for her then to have developed such strong feelings of rejection.

To reduce squabblings among siblings, each brother and sister should make every effort to be cooperative, kind and considerate. The thoughtfulness you show toward your siblings will help you develop good habits of friendliness toward others outside of your immediate family circle. Much sibling hostility and tension could be reduced if each sibling would carry his share of family responsibility instead of unfairly trying to unload his share upon the shoulders of another sibling.

If you are younger, don't become dependent upon your older sisters and brothers and expect them to pamper you; learn to stand on your own two feet and contribute your share toward sibling harmony. If you are older, don't bully your younger sisters and brothers; your problems and mistakes are not their fault, so don't use them as innocent victims upon whom to unleash your anger when you are unhappy. If you do this, you will feel more miserable later and your problems will still remain unsolved.

## RELATING TO RELATIVES

Another essential factor which causes differences in the personalities of siblings is the unique relationships of each sibling, not only with his parents and brothers and sisters, but also with others in his environment.

One child in a family may relate more readily to one relative or one family friend than do his brothers or sisters. This may have positive or, unfortunately sometimes, negative influences on this child or on other members of the family. Cathy's brother was born three months after their mother's brother had passed away, and he was named for his deceased uncle. The widowed aunt was delighted with his arrival, especially since he carried her departed husband's name. Cathy's birth a year and a half later brought no similar response. The aunt visited frequently and always brought gifts, expensive ones for Cathy's brother, inexpensive ones for Cathy.

The aunt's visits were a painful experience for Cathy. Her brother could do nothing wrong in the eyes of the aunt; Cathy, on the other hand, could do little right. Cathy's father viewed these visits with displeasure and, on several occasions, suggested to his wife that she, he and the aunt should sit down and have a heart-to-heart discussion on this matter.

He believed, correctly, that anyone visiting a family in which there is more than one child should bring equivalent gifts for each child (except on such special occasions as one child's birthday) or no gifts at all, but no one child should be favored to the neglect of the other child (or children). This latter is bad for the child who is favored as well as for the child who is neglected. Cathy's mother agreed with her husband's views, but refused to discuss the matter with the aunt for fear of angering her. Thus, this unfair and improper practice continued, and Cathy drowned her desolation in dinner desserts and other delicacies.

If something similar occurred in your life, remember that you, like Cathy, were the innocent victim of adult insensibility. It is easier to withstand a hurt when we know that it is not really intended for us. Cathy's aunt did not mean to hurt Cathy. The aunt did not understand children well enough to know that she was harming her nephew by her excessive gifts to him and that she was hurting Cathy by ignoring her.

## CHARACTER—CONSTRUCT WITH CARE

A great deal of our learning, especially during our early years, is by observation and imitation. Thus, young people frequently mirror the sociocultural setting in which they live. They reflect the adults they respect. They not only imitate their traits but also mimic their moral mores. This is the start of character development.

What is character? It is that part of your personality which consists of the basic set of values by which you live. It is your code of moral and ethical standards. These values and standards form the foundation of your character. They help you to differentiate between right and wrong as so judged by the society in which you live, and they are strengthened by the religious and spiritual teachings you receive at home.

The cornerstones for the building of character strength are respect, kindness, thoughtfulness and gratitude. All of the major religions preach the basic principle of the Golden Rule—do unto others as you want others to do unto you—and on this principle rests the foundation of good character.

Do you want others to be nice to you? Surely, you do. Well, then, are you quite sure that you have been nice to these others? Has someone been especially thoughtful and kind to you? Have you shown your gratitude to this person? Are you and your loved ones in good health? Are you grateful to the Good Lord for this good fortune?

Thoughtlessness, ingratitude, unkindness, inconsideration and disrespect are signs of poor, weak character. Sometimes children are inadvertently taught to be unkind or ungrateful or to act in a similarly discreditable fashion. Such is the case with Alice.

Alice's mother came from a fairly large family, most of the members of which are financially comfortable, but they have rarely, if ever, given Alice a gift. Alice's father's parents and his sisters and brothers are not as well off financially; however, despite their more limited finances, they have always given lovely gifts to Alice on her birthdays and other special holidays.

The contrast between the affection and attention of Alice's paternal relatives toward her and the absence of both affection and attention on the part of her maternal relatives has been marked indeed. As Alice was growing up, her mother found this situation very difficult to accept, and in an attempt to excuse her relatives' selfishness and to negate her in-laws' kindnesses, she often said to her daughter, "Those who have, give, and those who don't have, don't give."

This remark disturbed Alice very much, for she had hoped that her paternal relatives gave because they loved her (which they did) and not just because they "had." However, her mother's frequent repetition of this statement made her question her paternal relatives' true feelings toward her.

In an attempt to defend her brothers and sisters, Alice's mother unintentionally hurt and confused her daughter. How much better it would have been if Alice's mother could have accepted the situation realistically. She would have realized that her relatives felt insecure and unloved and that such people are often incapable of giving love, or of giving gifts as an expression of love, to others. Then Alice could have been able to accept and been strengthened by the love of her paternal relatives and could have given love and consideration to them in return.

Instead, Alice has grown to question the motives of those who love her and have been good to her, feels unloved, is unsure of herself and trusts no one including her parents. Her manners reflect her thoughtlessness and lack of gratitude toward those who have been kind to her.

## MANNERS MEAN MUCH

Character and manners are close kin. Your character is mirrored by your manners. Your internal code of ethics and your internal sense of values are expressed externally by your manners toward others. Character consists of all of your thinking and feeling about what is right and wrong; "manners" is doing what you consider to be right or wrong. Thus, just as good character development starts at home, so too do good manners.

If you don't say "Thank you" and "Please" to your parents and others at home, it is rather unlikely that you will do so to those outside your home. Despite poor manners, perhaps, you may yet rate high with your close relatives; but if you are ill-mannered to others, you will be judged as discourteous and ill-bred.

Stop for a moment and ask yourself this question, "Who was kind to me this week?"

Get a pencil and sheet of paper and start writing. List the names of those who have been thoughtful to you. To your surprise, this list will probably run much longer than you might have anticipated. Your parents head the list. They surely have been kind to you "over and beyond the call of duty" countless numbers of times during the week. And your grandmother. Didn't she bake especially for you those cookies you like so much? And your grandfather. Didn't he give you a few dollars to supplement your allowance, making it possible for you to buy that special sweater on sale at the local sportswear store?

Your Aunt Mary took you to the theatre to see that hit show which you otherwise would not have seen. And wasn't it nice of your uncle to give you that gift of a good, leakproof pen after he noted the ink stains on your fingers? Remember to add their names to your list.

Your history teacher excused you from the written test on Monday when you said you weren't feeling well and agreed to give you another test the following day, although this put him to the trouble of composing a special test for you. Then, there were your math teacher, your counselor, your club adviser, one of your neighbors, your friends—and there may be so many more you could add to this list of people who were especially good to you during this one, past week.

Now, stop again for a moment and ask yourself this other question, "Did I say 'Thank you' and, where called for, send a 'thank you note' to these people?" If you did, then you did well. If you didn't, it is not too late to get to work immediately on those verbal and written thank you's.

Having considered those who were nice to you, now, conversely, ask yourself if you offended someone recently. Did you say something hurtful? You wouldn't want anyone to offend you or hurt you, would you? Perhaps you just weren't feeling well that day or you weren't in a good mood or whatever your excuse might be (although there really isn't any *good* reason for hurting someone). Go ahead and apologize as quickly as possible. You'll feel better, and to some extent at least, you will ease the pain you inflicted on some innocent person.

One day, when Charlie was in the lower grades, he came home from school with a note for his mother asking her to report to the principal's office the following morning. Charlie had hit one of the boys in his class and torn his jacket. His teacher ordered him to apologize to the other boy, but Charlie refused. He was sent to the principal's office. The following morning, Charlie's mother was in school to see the principal, as he had requested. Although she found the principal's tale upsetting, as an intelligent woman and a competent, concerned mother, she knew he was right. Charlie had been weak and ailing as an infant and young child, and his mother, understandably under the circumstances, had been overprotective. Charlie had been permitted to say and do as he pleased because he was sickly.

Prior to this incident, Charlie's parents had noted many instances of misbehavior on Charlie's part, and they had become concerned that they were pampering him too much. They firmly believed in keeping the lines of communication open between parents and children and, therefore, held a family conference that evening at which Charlie was given the opportunity to state his side of the story. Next, Charlie's older brother, who was three years his senior and whom Charlie admired very much because he was the pitcher on the school's baseball team, said that he did not think Charlie was weak and that his parents should stop babying the younger boy and stop treating him as though he were a weakling.

Charlie's father stated that first Charlie must agree to apologize to his classmate the very next morning. He made it clear to Charlie that he was to apologize because he had been offensive and that he would not be given any reward for doing what was right, as had been done in the past. His mother reinforced this by adding that from this time forward Charlie was going to learn to behave properly and that proper behavior is its own reward. His parents stressed that impudence, inside and outside the home, would not be tolerated. They wanted him to understand why his act had been unacceptable and a family discussion ensued. Charlie agreed that he had been the aggressor and would apologize.

The parents agreed to permit Charlie to play ball and participate in other athletic activities if their family physician had no objections. Heretofore, Charlie had engaged in very limited sports for fear of catching cold or becoming breathless. The older brother volunteered to teach Charlie the rudiments of baseball. All agreed that participating in group sports would help Charlie to become more cooperative and more considerate of the rights of others.

Charlie learned about the importance of good manners at this family conference. He also learned something else of importance. He learned the value of having a calm discussion with his parents and older brother. The changes in Charlie did not take place within a fortnight, but his ability to communicate with the members of his family helped him to grow along more wholesome lines and to develop a more attractive, more positive personality.

## VENTILATE YOUR VIEWS

Many young people are not as fortunate as Charlie and complain that they cannot talk with their parents. Frequently, this is so because the young person is not making much effort to communicate with his parents and because the young person wants his parents to agree with him one hundred per cent of the time.

Often, when young people say their parents do not understand them, they mean their parents do not agree with them. First, you should accept the fact that your parents are your friends; if they do not agree with you, in all probability it is because they believe it is in your best interests for them not to agree. Second, in discussing matters with your parents, you should be ready to cooperate and to meet them at least halfway.

No matter what your parents did in the past which may have hurt you, remember that they did not set out to hurt you. Although, for example, Frankie felt that he had been rejected by his father, surely his father did not purposely reject him. There is a big difference between feeling and being. Thus, although Frankie felt rejected, no doubt his father would insist that Frankie had not been rejected. His father reacted, as best he could, to the changed circumstances in his life. Remember too that no matter how injurious may have been some of the experiences of your early childhood, rarely is anything so damaging that it cannot be rectified as you grow older and more mature.

To help you to mature, to aid you in rectifying anything that may need to be changed, it is vital that you ventilate your views. Sit down and talk with your parents. Strengthen your lines of communication with them. This does not mean that you must or should tell them everything. Everyone has some secret thoughts or information which he may wish to keep within himself; there are some things which we do not admit even to ourselves.

Ventilating your views does mean speaking with your parents as friend to friend, as confidant(e) to confidant(e); it means telling them what is troubling you, giving them your views, getting their views and benefiting from their greater knowledge and experience and from their special interest in you. It is a process of sharing with them for your mutual benefit.

As you strive to gain adult independence, you may hesitate and think it is a sign of dependence to discuss personal matters with your parents. On the contrary, it is a sign of confidence in yourself and in them.

The person who is unsure of himself is the one who finds it difficult and often impossible to seek advice from parents, from counselors, from teachers or from other knowledgeable older persons. As a truly dependent person, he attempts thus to camouflage his dependency and belittles the need for and value of parental advice and professional assistance.

It is an indication that you are on the right road to maturity if you can calmly communicate with your parents. So, go ahead, talk with them, listen to them and blend their views and thoughts with yours to enable you to come to your own decisions, which will be wiser ones because they will be based on this thoughtful communication.

# 5
# YOUR SECOND SOCIAL SETTING

YOUR SCHOOL ENVIRONMENT IS A MOST IMPORTANT environmental setting for you, second only to your home. When you entered kindergarten or went directly into elementary school, your teachers represented parent-substitutes, and it was necessary for you to adjust to these new authority figures. You made new friends among your schoolmates, and your social world became larger.

As you progressed onward through the elementary grades and into high school, you met more teachers and more schoolmates and made more friends. As your environment enlarged, so too did your interrelationships with people outside of your home.

Just as your parents and all others in your home environment have influenced your personality, so too have your past and present teachers, past and present schoolmates and the principals, counselors and all others who have been part of your total school environment. Similarly, just as your school activities affect your personality, so too does your personality affect your school activities.

## TEACHERS ARE PEOPLE TOO

You took a giant step forward on the road to maturity when you acknowledged that parents are people. Now take another step forward and concede that teachers are people too. Yes, they are. Perhaps there are one or two teachers in your past (or even present) with whom you have had some difficulties; think back now—and do try to be fair about it—did you cause any of these difficulties, or even if you did not, did you make efforts to meet your teachers at least halfway to clear up the trouble between you?

If you are having some disagreements with a teacher at present, ask that teacher for an appointment and discuss the cause of discord with him. Bear in mind that it is up to you to accommodate, compromise and be respectful.

Susie spent more time in her math class trying to catch her teacher in a mistake than in making an effort to learn from her teacher. One day, the teacher made a slight error in an equation which he had written on the blackboard. He stooped for an eraser to make the correction, but before he could do so, Susie shouted for all the class to hear, "You're wrong. The last number should be a three and not a two."

Susie got a momentary pang of pleasure by hurting her teacher, but the pleasure was short-lived; and like most indulged children (and Susie is still a "child," for although she is chronologically old enough to be called a young lady, she has not matured emotionally beyond the childhood stage of development), she sank right back into her usual sulky self. In the days and weeks that followed this incident, Susie continued to belittle her math teacher. It is an old psychological maxim that we find fault with those whom we have injured. It is also true that when we belittle others we really belittle ourselves.

Susie has a great deal of growing up to do. She must learn to mend her manners, to show respect for her teachers and to seek out the virtues instead of the shortcomings of others. Susie must learn that one gets respect by giving respect. If she wants others to forgive her for her imperfections (and she has many of them —everyone has some), she must ignore the faults of others (many of whom may have far fewer than she has); and if she wants others to notice her good qualities (and she has these too, as everyone has, but she keeps hers hidden from view), she should take cognizance of, and try to emulate, the good qualities of these others.

The more mature you are, the better you will understand that, in the main, teachers constitute one of the most dedicated groups of people. Of course, there are grouchy and grim teachers; there are grouchy and grim people, and teachers are people. Most teachers are determined to make available to you the best possible learning opportunities. However, learning is not a one-way process. You are not a vacuum or an empty container for a teacher or anyone else to fill with facts. You must participate; you must cooperate in the learning process. You must show an interest in the subject matter of your courses. If you resist your teachers' efforts to teach, you will not learn. You will get out of your courses no more than you put into them.

You may not be very pleased at present if you have strict teachers. Someday, however, you will be thankful that they played a part in your development. The strict teacher who makes you toe the line is helping you to become a more self-disciplined person. This self-discipline—more specifically here, intellectual discipline—is a precious personal possession. It will be of infinite aid to you later on in helping you to think more clearly, to make more logical decisions, to plan your daily programs more positively, and in a vast variety of other ways involving your school, family, job, social and community activities.

There is no more stimulating classroom atmosphere than one in which the teacher is ready and eager to teach and the students are receptive and yearning for learning. All right, you may say, you are interested and you do want to cooperate with your teachers, but there are certain subjects you must take which you simply do not like. What do you do then?

## SUBJECTS—SUBLIME AND STOLID

Well, it is true that not every subject is scintillating. Also, the subject which seems sublime to one student may seem stolid to another. You are not alone—if this is any comfort to you—in complaining about taking courses which are not to your liking; many students voice this complaint. Often, it has been found, students prejudge required courses.

Give them—and the teachers of those courses—and yourself a chance to get acquainted. Don't prejudge them. You may find, much to your surprise, that they are far more interesting than you had anticipated. Remember that required courses did not arise out of nowhere; experienced educators had good reasons for including them in the curriculum. If you persist in saying that there are certain courses you simply do not like and are unhappy at being compelled to take, then bear in mind that there are many things in life that we must do whether we like it or not.

It is a sign of maturity to accept with tranquillity those things we dislike, but which we haven't the power to change and must accept. Life is a process of constant adjustment, and this, all too often, includes adjusting to things and situations which may be unacceptable to us. It is better to learn and to accept this basic fact of life and become more adaptable when you are young, for it will give you greater strength and resiliency to confront any unexpected, unwelcome occurrences which may arise during your later adult life.

If your dislike for a specific subject is so strong, however, as to upset you severely, make an appointment to see your school counselor to determine where the difficulty lies. Perhaps in your case, there are certain extenuating circumstances which call for a change in program. It is well to remember, too, that your entire program of studies—the courses you like and those you may dislike—should meet with the approval of your school counselor. The courses you take should conform to the requirements for the type of diploma program in which you are enrolled.

There are three broad categories into which most high school curricula fall—namely, academic, commercial and vocational. The academic curriculum includes the college preparatory courses. The commercial and vocational curricula generally prepare the student for entry into the working world immediately upon receiving his high school diploma; there is a trend now for many commercial and vocational graduates to continue on to the two-year terminal curricula of the junior colleges or technical institutes.

Strive to do the best you can in your courses regardless of the curriculum you are undertaking. If you are having problems with any course, consult your school counselor. He will help you to find the cause of your problem and enable you to get the most out of each course. To derive the maximum benefits from your classes and for optimum learning, you must develop good study habits and good study skills.

## GO STEADY WITH STUDY

It is most important that you establish the habit of going steady with study. Studying is not something to be done just the night before an examination. It is a practice to be followed regularly every week of the school year.

Learning requires effort—more effort for some students and less for others and, likewise, more effort for some subjects and less for others, but effort nonetheless. The cramming that is done on the eve of an examination by those who have not studied on a regular periodic basis all through the term may help a student to pass a test, but it results in very little lasting learning.

Learning requires reinforcement. In Chapter 3 you were introduced to the human brain, and you became acquainted with the neuron connections, the synapses, across which nerve impulses pass. The impulses which arise from the thoughts which occur during the learning process, similarly, pass from one brain cell to another through these synapses. To learn, to acquire knowledge, to remember, we must strengthen these synaptic connections. This strength comes from reinforcement through regular study sessions.

Lasting learning, the kind of learning which will stay with you for many years, is the result of proper, periodic studying. One-time cramming before a test produces only weak synaptic connections; if you are fortunate, the facts which you have crammed into your brain will stay with you long enough for you to pass them on to your examination paper, but in all likelihood, you will have forgotten them within a week or possibly within a few days or even a few hours.

School is for learning and not just for the taking and passing of tests. We all have a great deal more intellectual potential— and all other potentials too—than we ever put to use. This potential cannot be activated and realized without knowledge, and study is necessary for the acquisition of knowledge. If you study properly and periodically, you will have little need to worry about passing examinations, you will learn your subject matter, and you will acquire knowledge. Knowledge is essential today to obtain gratifying employment, to become a constructive member of society and to live a meaningful life. Many students waste a great deal of time and do not learn as much as they should because of poor study habits.

Planning is the foundation for proper study habits. Plan your after-school hours to accommodate your homework and study requirements. You may have more homework in one course than in another, and you may need to spend more time studying one subject than another. Arrange your schedule to allocate sufficient time to meet your special needs.

On a clean sheet of paper, chart your study schedule for the week. List the hours of the day from early morning through the evening until your bedtime. Cross out the hours spent at school in both curricular and extracurricular activities. Then, considering each of the courses you are taking, map out the daily hours (or portions of hours) to be spent at homework and study for each course respectively. Allow for the time you will be devoting to home and family chores, to social-recreational activities and to miscellaneous personal functions and activities for which time must be allocated.

Have the determination to stick to your schedule, but yet allow for a degree of flexibility, for as you go along you may find that you need more time than you had anticipated for one subject and perhaps need less than you had planned for another. In this dynamic, rapidly changing world, flexibility is desirable in most other areas of life too.

A special, suitable place should be set aside for study purposes. Whether you have your own room or share a room, try to have some uncluttered, well-lighted, well-ventilated section where you are able to study without distractions. Radio, television and record players—and the telephone—are for before studying and after studying, but not for during studying.

Before seating yourself to study, be sure that on your desk or within easy access you have the necessary notebooks, textbooks, dictionary, paper, sharp pencils, pen and ink, eraser and any other supplies which you may need, such as a compass and ruler for math studies—and be sure you have attended to all essential physical and mental needs so you can work without interruption. Have a wristwatch or wall clock available to help you adhere to your schedule—and it will teach you the value of time. The chair on which you sit should be sturdy and suitable for your physical frame, but not so comfortable that you go to sleep soon after you have opened your notebook.

As you set about your studying, examine your assignment for the first subject on your schedule. Determine what is expected of you. Check the notes you took in class. Read the assigned pages of your text; reread more slowly and more attentively anything you may have failed to understand during the first reading. Carefully and concisely outline what you have read.

In your notebook, write the answers to the questions relating to your assignment, which you may find in your textbook or which your teacher may have given to you. Silently read your answers to the questions and your solutions to the assigned problems. Repeat them aloud. Review your notes and the material in the textbook. If anything puzzles you, write it down in your notebook and discuss it with your teacher the following day; he will be pleased to help you and will be happy to see that you are conscientious about his subject.

Take advantage of the priceless facilities available to you in your public library and school library. Develop the habit of reading good books for enjoyment and enlightenment. These libraries, in the main, are clean, quiet, comfortable places in which to read and study. The librarians are ready, willing and able to offer you their competent assistance; and additionally, the encyclopedias, atlases, reference materials and the many other books in these libraries should prove to be very useful to you in most—if not all —of your courses.

Dolores is a member of a large family; there is always noise and she could never find a quiet place for studying at home. She, therefore, got into the habit of doing homework and studying in the presence of what she considers "pleasant noise," the live television set. Doing homework or studying under distracting influences is highly undesirable, and by continuing to study in this manner, Dolores was establishing bad habits which are difficult to break. When her teachers and her school counselor noted that she was not doing as well as she should, this matter was discussed with her, and it was suggested that she spend more time in the school library and take fuller advantage of its facilities. Without distraction, in the wholesome atmosphere of the library, her study habits improved, and she has begun to make greater progress in her classes.

If you have been studying regularly and using all of the good school and library facilities available to you, you will not find it upsetting when any one of your teachers announces an upcoming examination. You will not need to cram. You will need to review the material which you have studied. After your teacher has told the class what the test will cover, you can decide which sections of the subject matter require more time for review and which require less. You will want to devote more time to reviewing those problems and questions which you find more troublesome.

On the eve of the examination, go to bed early to be relaxed and refreshed the next morning. Eat an adequate wholesome breakfast before leaving for school. Allow enough time to arrive in the examination room several minutes ahead of time. Be equipped with pen and ink, sharp pencils, eraser and any other necessary supplies. Be ready and alert to do your best.

Follow your teacher's instructions carefully and accurately. Write neatly and legibly; your answer may be correct, but if your teacher can't decipher what you have written, it won't do you very much good. Read each of your answers before you proceed to the next question and, as neatly as possible, make any necessary corrections. If you come upon a specially perplexing problem, skip it and continue on to the other questions; after you have completed the rest of the test, you can return to this problem, and its solution may then come to you more readily.

The students who do well in their classwork are frequently the ones who distinguish themselves too in school citizenship and participate actively in extracurricular activities.

## EXTRACURRICULAR ENRICHMENT

You need the intellectual nourishment provided by your program of studies. But to enrich your total personality and to get the fullest benefits of your school environment, you need too the social and recreational nourishment which comes from participation in your school's program of extracurricular activities. Your interactions and interrelationships with your fellow students help to build your poise and self-confidence.

When you were very young, your playmates were the little children who lived next door to you. Now, you have been making new friendships, based on similarities in interests, in ambitions, in personality traits, in ideas and ideals. You discover these similarities between yourself and your classmates in your classrooms and, to an even greater extent, in your extracurricular participation.

You and others like you may want to work on the school paper. Do you have any talent for editing or writing? Perhaps the editor-in-chief is looking for students who can edit or write articles or columns for the paper. Have you any art ability? The art editor may need you if you can draw. Would you like to sell advertising space in the paper to the local shopkeepers? If so, then you may be the one the advertising manager is seeking. Regardless of which task is assigned to you, participating in the paper's production will bring you into the company of other journalistic enthusiasts. This will enrich your social life and provide you with opportunities to learn how to get along harmoniously with others of your age level and older.

Perhaps journalistic endeavors have no appeal for you. Well, there are many extracurricular activities in which you may take part, and surely there must be one or more which you will find gratifying. If you are a camera fan and would like to learn how to take better photographs, you might want to join the photography club. And, speaking of clubs, no matter where your interest lies, there is bound to be at least one club that satisfies your wants. Most schools have a math club, a science club, an art club, an English club, a history club, foreign language clubs and ever so many more. So, take your choice. You'll make new friends, have loads of fun, and your personality will develop and flourish.

Are you athletically inclined? Perhaps you may be qualified to become a member of the football or basketball or baseball or volleyball or handball teams. If you can't make the team, perhaps you could join the cheering squad and help boost your team's morale. Do you like to battle with words and make public speeches? If so, the debaters' team was organized for people like yourself. Sharpen your wits, gather together your nouns and verbs, and join the scrap when your school debates an opposing team. Are you musically inclined? Do you play a particular instrument? Can you sing well? Then, you may be wanted by the school band or chorus. Report to the head of the music department and soon, perhaps, you will be rehearsing for the school's next big musical extravaganza.

Are you interested in the theatre? Like the Tender Ten, do you believe there is greasepaint in your blood? Well, then, go ahead and give your name to the president of the dramatics society or the drama club in your school. Perhaps you can act well enough to play a role in the annual or semiannual school show. If you cannot act, remember that there is need for more than actors and actresses in a play. There must be carpenters and artists to build props. Seamstresses and fashion designers are needed to make costumes. Admission tickets must be sold in advance, and this calls for a squad of aggressive student-salespeople. And, when the big day comes, quite a number of boys and girls must be ready to serve as ticket agents and ushers. There is a great deal that needs to be done, and surely you can find a task that will be suitable for you.

Your entire school program should consist of a wholesome combination of curricular and extracurricular activities in which neither is sacrificed to the advantage of the other. Your earnest application to your studies and eager participation in the extracurricular programs, each in its proper proportion, will help you to build a healthy, vigorous, positive personality. You will develop self-esteem and improve your confidence in relationships with others. You will also find positive, acceptable outlets for your creativity and imagination. Your curricular and extracurricular programs provide fertile fields in which your mental and special abilities may flourish.

## YOUR ABILITIES—MENTAL AND SPECIAL

Your total mental abilities are often referred to as your "intellectual capacity." This is better known as your "I.Q.," which, literally translated, means "intelligence quotient." Essentially, your I.Q. is an indication of your ability to learn and to solve problems.

There was a time—and it was not so very long ago—when it was believed that intelligence was *one* ability; it was thought that some people had a lot of this one ability, others had a moderate amount, and yet others had not very much. It was believed too that the amount of this ability which you possessed was constant throughout your life and that nothing could change it. Now, we know that this is not so. Intelligence is not *one* ability. It is more in the nature of a "package" composed of several different types of abilities. Then, too, we understand now that under certain favorable conditions, we can improve one, several or even all of these mental abilities which constitute this "package" known as intelligence.

There are a number of different mental abilities. Of special concern to you, for educational and career planning purposes, are the six primary mental abilities. These are (1) verbal comprehension ability, (2) word fluency ability, (3) spacial ability, (4) numerical ability, (5) reasoning ability and (6) memory.

Verbal comprehension ability is the power to grasp the meaning of what you hear and what you read. If you are above average in this ability, you find it easy to understand the ideas expressed in speeches, books, newspapers and magazines. If you have superior word fluency ability, you are able to express yourself readily and skillfully in writing and speaking.

Spacial ability is the capacity to see an object in all of its dimensions; some people are able to look at the drawing of a structure and visualize it in all of its height, depth and breadth. Some excel in numerical ability and are very competent in working with numbers. Reasoning ability is the facility which enables you to delve into problems and solve them logically. If you are especially capable of remembering lines for your school show or names, places and dates for your social studies courses, you may have a superior memory.

To understand yourself better, it is important for you to know in which of the mental abilities you are above average, in which you are average and in which you are below average. None of us is strong in everything. All of us have certain strengths and certain weaknesses. It is essential to determine which are your strong points and which are your weaknesses. This you can do with the assistance of your school counselor or school psychologist.

Additionally, it is important to know how you compare with others of your age level in your entire "package" of intelligence, your over-all intellectual potential. Your I.Q., your "general intelligence," is measured by an intelligence test, and undoubtedly you have taken a test of this type at some time in elementary school and again in high school.

The results of intelligence tests provide counselors and psychologists with information about your mental age (M.A.). To determine your I.Q., they divide your mental age (M.A.) by your chronological age (C.A.), your exact age in years, and multiply the result by 100. In equation form, this may be stated as follows:

$$\frac{\text{M.A.}}{\text{C.A.}} \times 100 = \text{I.Q.}$$

Thus, if you are seventeen and your mental age is seventeen, your I.Q. is 100. People with average general intelligence have I.Q.'s which are within the range of 90 to 110. If you are seventeen and your mental age is nineteen, your I.Q. is 112. This indicates that you have greater than average ability to learn, that you have greater intellectual potential than the average person your age.

In addition to your mental abilities, you possess certain other abilities known as "special abilities" or "aptitudes." These often are known also as talents. We all have talents of various kinds and of varying degrees. We may rank above average in certain aptitudes, below average in others and, probably, average in most. Some people have a great deal of art aptitude; others excel mechanically; others have superior musical or clerical or literary aptitude. The same person may excel in more than one special ability. The quantity and quality of talents differ with each person.

## YOU'RE GETTING TO KNOW YOU

The great Greek philosopher Socrates said, "Know thyself." All too often we may know more about others than we truly know about ourselves; it is easier for us to observe the behavior of others than it is for us to observe ourselves. At school, however, with the aid of your school counselor, school psychologist, teachers and schoolmates too, you have begun to learn and understand more about yourself.

In your classes, you have begun to determine which subjects you like and which you dislike, in which you excel and where you do poorly. You may not be especially interested in some of the subjects in which you are strongest. Interests and abilities do not always coincide. When they do, you can derive much benefit from this in your future career.

Your interests are uniquely yours. They are not necessarily similar to those of your parents, or your brothers and sisters, or your classmates or your friends. Your school subjects, your extra-curricular participation, your personality traits, your hobbies and your other spare-time activities provide excellent clues to your interests.

Somewhere in high school, you may have taken aptitude tests to determine the nature and degree of your aptitudes. Also, you may have received examinations known as "personality tests" and "interest tests." These are not "tests" in the generally accepted meaning of that word, for you cannot pass or fail them. Essentially, these are "inventories" which make it possible for the school counselor and school psychologist to determine your personality characteristics and your likes and dislikes more readily and more scientifically. There are a number of different personality examinations, some of which are administered on an individual basis and others on a group basis in the high schools and colleges.

In the high schools, the Kuder Vocational Preference Record is one of the most popularly used of the interest inventories. It lists numerous activities in groups of three, and the student is asked to indicate the one activity which he likes the most and the one he likes the least within each group. From the results, it is possible to determine your degrees of preference for the following vocational interest areas: outdoors, mechanical, computational, scientific, persuasive, artistic, literary, musical, social service and clerical. It has been found that most people have above average preferences for two or three interest areas, below average preferences for two or three others, and average inclinations toward the rest.

To determine scientifically your strengths and weaknesses, your mental and special abilities, your personality characteristics and your interests, consult your school counselor or school psychologist. We are living in a constantly changing world, and the understanding and knowledge which come from getting to know yourself better will help you to make wiser, more wholesome adjustments to these changes. It is, therefore, important that you now get to know and understand more about your feelings, your emotions.

What you put into school or into anything else depends to a great extent upon your emotions. Just what are the "emotions" and what is the meaning of being "emotional"?

# 6
# YES, YOU ARE EMOTIONAL

TREES DON'T LAUGH. PEOPLE DO. ROCKS DON'T CRY. People do. Animals and fish don't worry. People do. Why do people act this way? Because people are emotional.

Certain nonhuman vertebrates (the higher forms of animal and fish life which possess a spinal cord) are capable of some emotional experiences. Thus, for example, pets such as cats and dogs often express affection for their masters and fear or anger toward strangers. However, due to their restricted brain structures and lesser mental capacities, the range, quantity and quality of their emotions are exceedingly limited in comparison with those of humans. Our emotional capabilities and expressions are uniquely human.

During their ill-fated gathering, Alice accused Susie of being "emotional." All too often, people say to other people, "You're so emotional." Perhaps the frequent use of this statement has given you the impression that it is not good to be emotional. This is not so. Your emotions are your feelings. These feelings are a most important part of your existence.

## THE ESSENCE OF YOUR EXISTENCE

Emotions add essence to your existence. Without these feelings, you would be almost equivalent to a mechanical robot, and your

85

life would be drab and expressionless. With them, you are capable of being warm and human.

Yes, you are emotional—and be glad of it. But, although our emotions are desirable, distasteful displays of emotion are undesirable. Our emotions should be controlled and channeled into wholesome, socially acceptable avenues; they should not be excessively expressed nor improperly displayed in inappropriate places. Honest expressions of feelings are healthy and make for happier personalities.

As human beings, we love, we hate, we laugh, we cry, we are ecstatic, we are sad, we hope, we despair, we are bold, we are afraid, we are pleased, we are angered. There is a great range between such emotional displays as laughter and tears, love and hate, pleasure and pain. Some people laugh at the most trivial joke; from others, there is only a slight smile at even the most obvious humor. Some do not cry at the funeral of a loved one; others are moved to tears at the merest misfortune. In these and a number of other ways, we react to the world about us.

Our inner feelings are not always expressed to the outside world. Sometimes we keep them within us and wear a "mask" as the ancient Greek actors did. We may be angry, but we control this emotion and smile instead. We may be afraid, but we attempt to cover up this fear by "putting on an act" of bravery. There are times when it is wise and healthy not to express our feelings directly, but to release them into other channels; it is unwise and unhealthy to "bottle up" our emotions and keep them unreleased.

The expression of your emotions and their nature and degree are controlled by your brain. Individuals differ in their mode and manner of emotional expression. Some people have more emotional breadth and/or emotional depth than others. There are those who are capable of having affection and compassion for a great many people, including even people whom they do not know personally but may have read or heard about; others can have positive feelings for only an exceedingly few people who are very close to them. The emotional breadth of most people may be found somewhere between these two extremes.

Similarly, there are those who feel very deeply and very intensely; when they like someone, for example, there are great depth, strength and sincerity in this feeling. Others feel only on a rather superficial level and may be quite unresponsive. Again, as with emotional breadth, the emotional depth of most people ranges somewhere in the center of these more extreme forms of expression.

In spite of the differences in the individual intensity and scope of our feelings, all of us have sufficient emotional capacity to add meaning and exhilaration to our lives. It is indeed a rare person who is emotionally impotent. Just as with our mental capacities, so too we use only a small portion of our emotional potentialities during our lifetime. Thus, our emotional problems are less concerned with how much emotional potential we possess, but are a great deal concerned with where to express our emotions, how to express them and how to control them when they need controlling.

Although it is believed that constitutionally we all have different emotional potentials, our emotional growth and development depend essentially upon all that happens to us from the very day we are born. We respond to the emotional behavior of others, and others, in turn, respond to our emotional behavior toward them. Our individual emotional progress and our future emotional security depend very much upon the quality and quantity of emotional warmth which we received when we were quite young.

Our ability to express our emotions starts at an early stage in our lives, and the kind and amount of feelings which we continue to exhibit are directly related to the emotional behavior which others have shown toward us. As we grow older and, hopefully, acquire additional maturity, we tend to learn how to control our emotions, into which channels to direct them, when to release them and how to use them to our fullest advantage.

Love, anger, fear and grief are considered to be the most powerful of our emotions. It has long been known that air, food, clothing and shelter are basic essentials of life. We now know too that love is an additional essential for a child's wholesome development and growth.

## LOVE IS A MANY MISJUDGED THING

Love is probably the most misunderstood and misjudged emotion, and the word itself is probably the most misinterpreted and misused word in the English language. Love, the most basic and most powerful of all the emotions, is expressed in varied acts of kindness and consideration toward others, acts which have very little relationship to the Hollywood version of the word "love." True love is the devotion, respect and tenderness we give to someone because of our strong, positive feelings of affection toward that someone.

There are many different kinds of love. There is love for one's mate and children, for parents, for grandparents, for sisters and brothers, for other relatives, for friends and, certainly too, for pets. There is also the tremendous affection and loyalty—and this too is love—which one has for an alma mater, for a group or an organization to which one belongs, for a hometown, for one's country, for humanity, for nature, for God.

Love may range from the slightest bit of affection for a stranger who accidentally crosses our path and performs a simple act of kindness, to the deepest devotion and respect for a cherished mate, child, parent or other close relative or friend.

Babies thrive on affection. Being fondled and hugged by their parents produce feelings of pleasure within them, and they gurgle, laugh and hug in return. When a baby does not receive what he wants, he becomes frustrated and cries out in anger.

Some babies may appear to be more ill-disposed and less affectionate than others, and their parents should be especially warm and understanding to bring out the tenderness in them.

Every child needs to feel that he is loved. He needs to be cuddled, comforted and cared for by his parents. The affection and attention, the warmth and well-being which he receives from his parents inform him that all is well with his world. As the child grows older, he needs a helping hand to hurdle the years of childhood and adolescence. His parents' assurance, encouragement and guidance are essential to him. Some children need more encouragement than others, and parents should use their judgment in giving to each child according to his needs.

The baby and young child need to *be loved*. Although they react to the love which is bestowed upon them with joy, laughter, hugs, kisses and other individual responses, they must develop and grow before they inwardly feel the emotion of love toward those who love them. Thus, the child develops from being *a receiver of love*, one who needs very much to be loved, to *a giver of love*, one who creates love within himself and can give this love to his mother and father.

As he grows older, if he is maturing along wholesome lines, the child begins to conquer his egocentricity (his concern chiefly with himself) and is able to give love to others beyond his parents. He begins to find more satisfaction in giving than in receiving. He learns that love involves giving as well as getting, that it involves a mutual sharing. He is able to move from sole concern with self to concern for the needs of others and to show devotion and thoughtfulness to all who have been kind to him even beyond his inner family circle.

There are some people who are capable of intense feelings of love, in breadth and in depth—love for their mate and children, for their parents, for other members of their family, for their friends, for their country, for humanity and for God. There are others who do not have as much breadth or depth of feeling, and their love, even for a mate to whom they may have been long married, is not very strong; instead, it is a limited loyalty to someone with whom they have been long acquainted. The most wonderful and remarkable quality of this powerful emotion, love, is that the more you give of it, the more is generated within you to continue to give.

Children who grow up in an atmosphere of love, where their parents love each other and love their children, develop emotional security which fortifies them to manage the fortunes and misfortunes of modern life. Such is the atmosphere in Charlie's home. Charlie has problems, as all people his age and all people of all ages have. However, strengthened by the self-respect and self-esteem which his parents helped him to develop, he is capable of communicating with them and is able to cope with his problems in a manner which manifests exceptional maturity for one his age.

The child who does not receive the warmth and affection he needs may grow up feeling rejected and be rebellious toward society. This is true of Frankie. With Alice there has been confusion, and she has been torn between her parents. Although occasional discord and disagreements are perfectly normal in a relationship as close as that between a husband and wife, the quarrels between Alice's parents are excessively frequent and Alice shudders in her room each time she hears the word "divorce" during these quarrels. Alice told her minister that hers was not as yet a "broken home," but that she felt that it was a "cracked home" and that the "crack" was bringing bruises to her daily.

Alice was wise to discuss her problem with her clergyman, for he can help her and her parents. Often children have been able to assist in reconciling the differences and dissensions between their parents, and Alice may be able to accomplish this with the aid of her minister. The frictions and frustrations of such childhoods as Alice's need not be permanently damaging, although they do tend to produce poor personality patterns. However, with the help of her minister and her school counselor, Alice will be assisted in the process of replacing these negative patterns of behavior with positive acceptable behavior patterns.

## THE RAGES OF ANGER

When a very young child does not get what he wants when he wants it, he may shout, scream or cry as a means of exhibiting his feelings of anger. If he is further frustrated, he may have a temper tantrum.

Some parents, with all good intentions, fearful of frustrating their child and upset at the sight of the tantrum, immediately yield to the child's wishes. Thus starts a bad behavior pattern wherein the child uses the temper tantrum as a tool to get whatever he wants. Unfortunately for them, some children carry this form of behavior into adulthood. They then discover, to their surprise, that this is not effective as a means of getting what they want from adults other than their parents. Instead, they find that other people are repulsed by this behavior.

Susie often resorts to temper tantrums. Since Susie is an only child, her parents, especially her father, have treated her as though she were a very royal princess. Every wish of Susie's is her daddy's command. Her father means well, but fails to realize that he is indulging in love for himself rather than love for his daughter. When he gives her everything she desires, regardless of whether it is good or bad for her, he hinders her wholesome progress to adulthood.

Anger wells up within Susie when she is denied her wishes outside of her home, and she is unable to restrain her temper. When her schoolmates refused to accept her ideas, she shouted and told the chairman what she thought of him.

Anger may extend from slight annoyance to an outburst of rage with many levels of irritation and resentment in between. There are times in the lives of each of us when we may be overcome by feelings of hostility; perhaps someone has done us a grave injustice, or perhaps we feel fate has treated us unfairly.

There is never any justification, however, for foisting our fury on innocent people and causing harm to them. The inability to restrain oneself is a sign of immaturity. There are acceptable outlets for this wrath which wells up within us when we become angry at someone or something.

Are you angry at fate or foe? Do some exercise. Go for a walk. Slam away at a ball in a game of tennis, golf or handball. Beat all of the dust out of that old rug in the attic. Pound on that powerless punching bag. You will feel much better after engaging in any one of these activities—or you may have some favorite physical outlet of your own which you may prefer.

By releasing your anger through these innocuous outlets, you will ease the many harmful side effects which anger has on so many parts of the body, and you will not have (1) mistreated your parents, who were undeserving of this mistreatment, (2) insulted your boss and lost your job as a consequence, if your boss was the cause of your anger, (3) attacked your friend and threatened your friendship, if the friend aroused your anger, or (4) unfairly inflicted pain on some innocent person upon whom you may have vented your anger simply because, unfortunately for that person, he was within your reach at that moment.

Although love is a positive emotion, anger, as indicated, often can be negative. Anger has provoked people to acts of violence and crime. However, anger does have its positive aspects too. In addition to releasing your anger in directions where it can be neutralized and can do a minimum of harm to yourself and to others, you can also direct the emotional energies generated by anger into positive pathways for many productive purposes.

Anger at cruelty, poverty, prejudice and other injustices has provoked many people to use their time, efforts and physical energies in addition to their emotional energies to combat these injustices. Teen-agers and adults alike have become incensed at improprieties and inadequacies in their city or county governments. As a consequence, they have campaigned conscientiously for the candidates of their choice, who they believed were most capable of improving and correcting the improper conditions.

## FACING UP TO FEARS

All of us are afraid at some times in our lives. Some are more easily intimidated and are more afraid more often of more people and more things; others are more daring and less afraid. Fear is a good and normal reaction to danger when there is a sound basis for the fear. If a tiger escaped from a local zoo and a radio announcer informed us that the tiger was headed for the street on which we live, we would be justified in being afraid to go out into the street until the tiger had been captured.

Babies are afraid of falling and of loud noises. These two fears are classified as instinctive (inborn responses) by many psychologists. As they grow older, babies may be afraid of strange faces and may cry in fear if someone they do not know tries to hold them. Later, the child may gather many other fears depending upon those of his parents and others around him. His own personal experiences will build or banish fears. Thus, a young child who was scratched by a cat may, thereafter, be afraid of cats. The child whose mother is afraid of dogs may learn to be similarly afraid. With increased age, the child may abandon some of his childhood fears, perhaps replace them with others or hold onto them and add others.

It is a sign of intelligence to be afraid when the situation calls for fear. A woman who is walking alone on a darkened street late in the evening has cause to be afraid. We would question her basic good sense if she were not afraid. This fear is good for it helps to protect her. It puts her on guard and causes her to be more cautious. It also brings about certain physiological (functional) reactions within the body. Her heart beats faster. Her glands are activated. All of the systems within her body become more alert to give her greater power and strength in case any potential danger which may lurk on a darkened street should become an actual danger.

Fear is a powerful emotion, but we must be careful to see that it does not overpower us. We must face up to our fears to determine what it is that we fear and why we fear it. If we let ourselves be overcome by fear, especially when that fear has little if any rational basis, we may find ourselves unable to act or react as sensibly as we otherwise might. When fear overpowers us, it can paralyze mind and muscle and prevent us from doing what should be done.

Eddie's mother is afraid to fly. She has never been in an airplane and insists that she never will enter one. Although she has read newspaper stories of plane accidents, she has never known personally anyone who was injured in a flight accident. Eddie's father has argued frequently with his wife and offered many valid reasons why she should fly with him on his trips rather than use any other form of transportation, but to no avail.

She is deaf to all of his statements that the number of people who are killed and injured in automobile accidents annually is greater than the number of plane deaths and injuries. Facts have no effect upon her; she simply will not fly. This then is an irrational fear (see *phobias* below), and it would require professional probing to discover the underlying cause (or causes). Irrational fears may bring about many personal and family problems. Although Eddie's mother's fear does not do too much damage to the family's basic way of life, it does prevent the father from doing certain things as he would prefer.

Fear has many related forms, and included among these, in their varied intensities, are worry, anxiety and the phobias. *Worry* is the state of uneasiness and apprehension which results from an expectation of danger. It is perfectly normal to worry, especially when there is a real basis for anticipating trouble. It becomes a psychological problem when the worry is excessive and prolonged, when it impedes an active attack on the problem which is causing the worry, and when there may not be a fundamental, rational reason for expecting problems or dangers to arise.

*Anxiety* is a state of intense, chronic worry. It may range from milder to more severe forms and, with it, bring varied internal bodily disorders, such as high blood pressure, digestive disturbances, irritability, weakness, fatigue, depression and an inability to cope with reality.

The *phobias* are extreme fears which are tenacious and irrational in nature. There are many different kinds of phobias, and among the more common ones are acrophobia, fear of heights; agoraphobia, fear of open places; ailurophobia, fear of cats; claustrophobia, fear of closed spaces; cynophobia, fear of dogs; monophobia, fear of being alone; mysophobia, fear of dirt and germs; ochlophobia, fear of crowds; panphobia, fear of everything; and xenophobia, fear of strangers.

## THE GAMUT OF GRIEF

Sorrows affect different people in different ways. In times of intense grief, such as the death of a loved one, there are those who give an outer appearance of stoic calmness and remain comparatively dry-eyed, whereas others shed torrents of tears. Similarly, a trivial frustration may bring forth outbursts of sadness from some, whereas a major catastrophe may bring only an externally limited, restrained response from others.

Grief ranges from the slightest sorrow to the direst disappointment, to the most treacherous throes of tremendous tragedy. The way we react in times of grief depends not only upon our individual capacities for emotional breadth and depth, but also on our innermost feelings and attitudes toward the one for whom we are grieving. The fact that one person does not shed a tear and that the other person sheds many does not necessarily mean that the second is more grieved than the first;

on the contrary, sometimes the one who cries the least may be the one who is most grieved, and the one who cries most copiously may be the least grieved.

Each one has his personal way of reacting to grief. We should not judge the degree of another person's sorrow on the basis of his outward expressions of grief. Some people who do not cry are sincerely sorrowing; others who do not cry are truly unmoved by the tragedy. Some who cry copiously are deeply grieved; others who cry are not at all marred or moved but are "putting on an act" because they believe this "act" is required of them.

All too often, unfortunately, sons and daughters who weep voluminously at the funeral of a parent, and wives or husbands who do likewise at a mate's funeral, are moved less by grief and more by guilt feelings. These feelings of guilt result from not having been as kind and thoughtful to the departed as these mourners might have been. *Guilt feelings* are not the same as guilt. *Guilt* implies wrongdoing or violation of a law. The person suffering from guilt feelings, however, need not necessarily be guilty. This person is troubled by feeling what he did was wrong or that what he did caused something bad to happen. Often such a person needs professional help to make him understand that he may not have done wrong and to enable him to live at peace with himself.

Throughout his young life, Billy had heard his parents constantly disagreeing. One morning, they had another of their many unpleasant clashes. His father quietly closed the door behind him and proceeded out to the corner bus. He never reached the bus stop sign. He collapsed of a heart attack some fifty feet from his front door. Billy has been in silent sorrow since that sad spring day.

Six weeks later, Billy's mother signed a lease for an apartment in another part of town, and Billy was transferred to the school in his new neighborhood at the end of the school term, which was then drawing to a close. At his new school, Billy feels the sorrow not only of the loss of his father but also of the loss of his old friends, classmates and neighbors.

Billy told his family physician that his mother cries constantly, but, he added, he is not sure whether she is crying because she has nobody to fight with or because she really loved his father despite all the battles. It was unfortunate that his mother decided to move so soon after her husband's death, thus causing a second upheaval in Billy's life. It is fortunate, however, that Billy has a good relationship with his family physician, who can be of great help to him in this troubled period of his life.

## THE GREEN-EYED MONSTER

In addition to the numerous variations and gradations within the four basic emotions of love, anger, fear and grief, there are a multitude of other emotions, such as bewilderment, frustration, inferiority, insecurity, jealousy, joy, pain, pleasure and a great many more. Of these, jealousy is the most corrosive and is often called the "sick emotion."

In *Othello*, Shakespeare refers to jealousy as "the green-eyed monster which doth mock the meat it feeds on."

Jealousy is truly a "monster" which consumes the jealous person's time, energies and general well-being. There are those who are jealous of someone else's fancier car, better clothes or larger allowance. If these same people were somehow suddenly to acquire similarly fancier cars, better clothes or handsomer allowances, they would still continue to suffer from the pangs of jealousy, except that now the jealousy would focus on some other items, such as someone else's new record player or some other material thing.

Jealousy is an indication of internal discontent and feeling of personal worthlessness. The jealous person is plagued by a low opinion of himself. Jealousy is not dependent upon whether you have any particular tangible items or material possessions.

It is dependent upon your feeling of self-esteem. The only insurance against jealousy is the possession of the feeling of wholesome self-worth.

Become aware of your own fine qualities and features. Surely there is something about yourself of which you can be justly proud. Accentuate your many positive attributes and your outstanding characteristics. You will be less apt to be resentful of what others have or what others do if you have a vigorous sense of self-worth and self-esteem. You will not begrudge others their successes if you are pleased with your own positive accomplishments.

You are capable of achievement. You do have specific exceptional traits. No one excels at everything; but all of us do have certain distinctions and attainments which can enhance our feelings of personal worth. Each of us has the capacity to achieve in some area. Some students do superior work in mathematics; others in English literature or in biology, history, Spanish, economics, automobile mechanics and so on. Some people are especially competent at building model airplanes; others are proficient at baking cakes or fixing television sets or singing in front of large audiences or playing a musical instrument.

Everyone has at least some one thing which he can do better than most other people can. Realize your own potential, bring it to fruition, accomplish that for which your abilities and aptitudes qualify you, and jealousy will be far less likely to prey upon you. Those who have a mature, humble sense of self-satisfaction can have respect and admiration for the accomplishments of others and will not fall victim to jealousy.

## CONTROLLING YOUR FEELINGS

Your emotions must often be restrained. You must learn to control your feelings instead of letting your feelings control you. You may be angry at your teacher or hate your employer, but it would not be very wise or mature to vent your fury on either person.

Bottling up your emotions within you, however, can be a great threat and very damaging to your health. Mounting anger, anxieties, disappointments, fear and hatred stimulate the adrenal glands to secrete more adrenalin. This increases the blood pressure, causes the heart to beat faster and prepares the body to respond more readily to an outer threat. If the body does respond, the pressures are dissipated and the internal organs return to normalcy. If not, the blood pressure remains high and serious damage may be done to the heart, stomach, kidneys and other vital organs.

As the emotional pressures rise, if they are not released in a wholesome fashion, they may bring on a dangerous outburst or an emotional explosion injurious to the person himself and, often too, to innocent victims in his environment.

Dolores' father had hoped to receive a promotion at his place of employment. Instead, the coveted higher position was given to a subordinate of his. The day he learned of this injustice, he was full of resentment and hostility. He worried about his future with the company. Anger, fear, sorrow, insecurity, envy and the fury of his other furtive feelings fumed within him. He said nothing to his supervisor and wore a brave smile to cover his hurt feelings. To his co-workers, he said that he had not really expected to be promoted, that he did not as yet deserve it and, therefore, was not at all disappointed; all of which was, of course, just the reverse of the truth.

When the working day was over, he hated to face his wife. He had a large family to support and needed the extra income the promotion would have brought with it. Seething with anger, he entered his car. He stepped on the gas, and within a few moments, he crashed into the car in front of him. The driver of the other car landed in the hospital with multiple injuries. Dolores' father was critically injured, but fortunately recovered after a three-month stay in the hospital.

If Dolores' father had better control over his emotions, he would have faced up to the reality of the situation. He would have been wise to have spoken with his firm's personnel director to determine why he had been bypassed and what he could do to insure his promotion at the earliest possible date.

If a man is unhappy at his work and is overcome by feelings of frustration, how much better it would be if he visited the counseling center at his local college or university, or an approved counseling agency or a certified counseling psychologist. A counselor or psychologist would help him to decide whether he should remain on his present job, whether he should seek more suitable employment, or whether he would profit from further education, retraining or specialized training.

Dolores' father expressed his feelings and released his resentment, but he did so in a most unwholesome, most disastrous manner. He discharged his emotional energies into destructive rather than constructive pathways, thus causing injury to an innocent man and to himself. It is important that we release our emotions and not permit them to build up to explosive proportions. We must be careful, however, that we direct them into wholesome, constructive outlets, outlets which do no harm to ourselves or to others.

## YOUR "SAFETY VALVES"

Look at the hot-water and steam boiler in your private or apartment house. You will note that there is a safety valve which permits some of the steam to escape before the pressure inside the boiler reaches the danger point. Human beings also need "safety valves," and we have them in the form of many healthy outlets.

Charlie was unhappy about many of the things which took place at the meeting of the Tender Ten, but he did not belittle or shout at any member of the group. Instead, he offered good constructive criticism and advice. Then, he left for the gym where he would release in a sound, sensible manner the emotional pressures which welled up within him during the meeting.

Each person must seek out those constructive, positive outlets ("safety valves") which are most suitable to his personality and to the particular problem which he is facing. Two of the most effective safety valves for the discharge of our emotions are walking and talking. A vigorous walk is a valuable way to give off "steam" and reduce the inner pressures. Talking is helpful too if it is done in a thoughtful manner with a parent, teacher, school counselor, psychologist, psychiatrist, family physician, clergyman or other capable, concerned adult who would not divulge any confidences.

Other healthy outlets for your emotional energies are physical exercises, participating in sports, fighting for community causes, learning to play a musical instrument, painting, being a participating member in worthwhile organizations, engaging in hobbies or any one of a multitude of beneficial activities which effectively ease your tensions.

Instead of seeking release for their emotional pressures through sound safety valves and then standing up to their problems realistically, many people employ certain mental mechanisms which may relieve their anxieties and reduce their tensions temporarily but do not solve their problems. In this manner, they try to protect their ego-integrity and defend their "self."

# 7
# YOUR "SELF" DEFENSE

LOOK AT YOURSELF IN THE MIRROR. WHOM DO you see? YOU!

But WHO are YOU? In addition to the several yous with whom you have now become acquainted, the mirror introduces you to more of YOU. A full-length mirror reflects your height, your girth (indicating your approximate weight), the contour of your face, the slant of your eyes, the size of your nose, the shape of your mouth, the bend of your ears, the color of your skin, the length of your feet and a variety of other discernible physical characteristics.

Each of these characteristics has an effect on your total personality. Surely you know people who are sensitive because they believe that their ears bend too far forward or their nose is too large or their eyes are too small or some other feature simply is not what they would like it to be. Millions of people have suffered indignities and inequalities due to the color of their skin. Many others have sustained psychological distress due to physical disabilities. All of these have entered into the molding of their individual personalities.

Billy is sensitive about his lack of height, and this has aggravated his shyness. Billy has numerous talents. He plays the piano exceptionally well. He excels in constructing model aircraft. He should join the school orchestra and the hobby club, where his talents would be recognized and applauded. This acceptance by his classmates and teachers would build his self-confidence, help to make him a more outgoing individual, cause him to pay greater attention to his adequacies and abilities ànd less to his in-adequacies, and thus reduce (and, hopefully, eventually elimi-nate) his sensitivity about his size. Billy should also be told that during the high school years, many boys sprout up and add a number of inches to their height, and this could happen to him.

All of these aspects of your personality—your physical char-acteristics plus the anthropological, biological, cultural-environ-mental, intellectual, emotional and mental factors—are inter-woven and interrelated. We have been examining them sepa-rately here to enable you to get a better view and understanding of each factor, but in the actual functioning of your personality all of these factors are inseparable and interconnected.

Also, your total personality in its composite form—your total "self"—is greater than the sum of all of these factors. Surely there are certain individuals you know about whom you say, "He's such an all-around good fellow," or "She's just so nice." You do not stop to analyze, nor do you care, whether it is their thoughtfulness or their sense of humor or their cheerful attitude or whatever other positive factor it is which attracts you to them; you do know that as total beings—as total "selfs"—you find them to your liking.

## YOUR MANY "SELFS"

You are a living, thinking, reasoning, feeling human being— a dynamic, growing, changing self. As you look in the mirror and stare at your physical characteristics, you may reflect too upon your total being, your "self." Your "self" is the individual YOU, the YOU which distinguishes you from all other human beings. Human beings, however, are very, very complex, as has been indicated, and you as a human being are very, very complex. Thus, there is no single "self."

You are a number of "selfs." Your *actual self* is the person you really are; but remember that with time and circumstance, you keep changing and so your actual self keeps changing too. Your *ideal self* is the person you would like to be. Your *assumed self is* the one you think you are. Your *social self* is the person others think you are.

Your actual self often strives to convert the person you really are and the one you think you are into the one you would like to be and the one you would like others to think you are. The pressures of mid-twentieth-century existence, however, are many, and frequently the actual self has difficulty enough maintaining its ego-integrity, its self-esteem.

Self-acceptance, self-confidence and self-esteem are essential for your emotional security and inner strength. We all have our positive characteristics (strong and good points) and our negative characteristics (weak and poor points). We must make an effort to bring out and accentuate our acceptable traits and make a similar effort to reduce or rid ourselves of the unacceptable ones.

The esteem which others have for you may be multiplied by your improving and increasing your positive points. This esteem, bestowed upon you by others, will help build your self-esteem, which in turn will elevate your self-confidence. The reduction and/or destruction of your negative points will tend to make you more acceptable to others, bringing greater self-acceptance to you, and this similarly will augment your self-confidence.

## YOUR "SELF" AND SOCIETY

The many stresses which society often imposes upon us and the numerous urgencies and tensions thrust upon us by family, friends, school, employer, community and the world at large may, at times, attack our confidence and threaten our actual self.

A stressful situation may make us irritable, uneasy, fatigued and impatient with even petty impediments which would be tolerable under normal circumstances. If we encounter distress and defeat and continue to find obstructions in the pathways toward our goals, we may become frustrated.

*Frustration* is the state of extreme disappointment which results when obstructions prevent us from achieving our goals or from satisfying our needs. Some people have greater ability to withstand frustrations than others. Thus, some may meet many major disappointments and yet persist along their determined paths; they are said to have *high frustration tolerance.* Others surrender or succumb to a most minor discomfort; they have *low frustration tolerance.* Some people anticipate frustration and suffer from anxiety.

*Anxiety,* as indicated in the preceding chapter under the section "Facing Up to Fears," is continued intense worry. It is a state of mental misery caused by the anticipation of trouble. Anxious people look out upon society and the world in which they live with a dread of the future due to an expectation of danger from unknown sources. In the main, anxious people suffer from feelings of inadequacy and unworthiness; they view themselves as not as acceptable or as estimable as others, and are not well adjusted to the society of which they are a member.

Your actual self is in constant interaction with society and often in conflict with it. These conflicts are many times accompanied by frustration and anxiety. The latter bring with them many discomforts which are upsetting to your self, and your self then struggles to overcome these discomforts.

## DEFENDING YOUR "SELF"

In its battle to defeat the discomforts of frustration and anxiety, your self is striving to defend its self-esteem and to protect its ego. How does it do this? Well, the best way would be to confront realistically the conflict which faces you and to cope with and conquer it in as satisfactory a manner as possible.

Oftentimes, however, people cannot or will not face up to their problems and are unable to come up with adequate solutions to these problems. Instead, these people have discovered certain tension-reducing techniques which allay their anxieties and diminish their discomforts. These behavioral techniques help them to justify many of their personal inadequacies or to flee from any real or illusory threat and enable them to cope at least temporarily with their tension-ridden environment.

These same behavior mechanisms or mental devices, as they are also known and of which there are many varied forms, may be performed on the conscious level where you are aware of what you are doing to defend yourself, or they may be performed on the unconscious level where you are unaware of the device you are using to protect your ego. When these devices are discharged on the unconscious level, they are known as *defense mechanisms*.

Defense mechanisms are used to aid a person in his quest for a reprieve from a stressful situation. Instead of realistically attacking the emotional conflicts which confront him, a person may have gotten into the habit of employing these defensive processes, and thereafter when a conflict arises, a specific mechanism (an intrapsychic process operating on the unconscious level) automatically comes into action to aid him in coping with that conflict.

Some of these mechanisms employ mental flight to help an individual avoid having to face reality, and these are known as *escape mechanisms*. The escape mechanisms take varied forms of flight and evasion, such as *postponement, fantasy, regression* and *repression*. Among the other varieties of defense mechanisms are *dissociation, denial, rationalization* and *compensation*.

## ESCAPE MECHANISMS

Escape mechanisms are defensive processes which enable people to evade reality by mentally fleeing from frustration or other anxiety-producing conditions. There are those people who constantly postpone until "tomorrow" doing something which should be done today. "Tomorrow," for them, is in the very far-off future, if ever, and not a real tomorrow.

*Postponement,* for those who are not fully aware that they are using this defensive process, is an escape mechanism used as a means of fleeing into the future. For them, this is a future forever postponed, and thus they avoid coming to a head-on collision with an issue which cries out for immediate resolution, but which they are unable to resolve. Cathy has often said she would start dieting "next Saturday"; although Saturday appears regularly each seventh day, for Cathy "next Saturday" has not come as yet.

*Fantasy* is an imaginary state wherein all desires are delivered and all distresses disappear. Daydreaming is a popular form of fantasy. Some daydreaming on a conscious level is useful as a healthy release from the tensions of daily life. It may serve too as an incentive and stimulate the daydreamer on to greater achievement. However, excessive daydreaming on the unconscious level may result in removing the daydreamer from the realm of reality. It becomes detrimental when the daydreamer receives so much pleasure from imaginary events that these replace the need for real accomplishments and real action.

Dolores finds rich rewards in her fantasy states. Surrounded by pessimistic people at home, she finds in fantasy satisfying events in which everything turns out well and nothing is disastrous. During the meeting of the Tender Ten, Dolores sat and daydreamed of the grand role which she would play in this project, but she offered no constructive ideas. When the meeting ended in ruins, she was there to state that this was what she had expected. How much better it would have been, for her and for the others, if she had actively participated, quietly stated her views and done her part to prevent the meeting's collapse.

*Regression* is a defensive process in which a person reverts to patterns of behavior which are typical of an earlier stage of de-

velopment. Thus, a person who is past his majority and, therefore, chronologically an adult may regress, especially in times
of serious illness, to infantile ways and seek to be babied and
pampered.

Regression is not the same as *retrogression,* which sounds similar. Whereas regression means a return to a *pattern of reacting*
which is *typical of an earlier age level,* retrogression is a retreat
to a *specific act* performed by a specific person when he was
younger; thus, the person who was a nail-biter when he was
very young is said to be retrogressing when, as an adult in a
time of severe emotional conflict, he returns to nail-biting. *Fixa-
tion* is the arrest of a person's emotional growth, resulting in his
failure to mature beyond one of the early stages of development.

*Repression* is a means of maintaining one's self-respect by ex-
cluding from one's consciousness any acts, experiences or ideas
which are unpleasant and/or unacceptable to us. Eddie's father
is an alcoholic who had succeeded in controlling this problem
and had not had a drink for almost five years. In a sober state,
he is a man of dignity and decorum. Recently, the pressures rose
and the temptations were considerable. Eddie's mother had been
urging her husband to accept a business proposition which was
unacceptable to him because it had certain shady aspects to it.

One morning recently, Eddie's mother harassed her husband
mercilessly for not earning more money, in spite of the fact that
his income is a good deal above average; she cruelly compared
him with his brother who had just given his wife a full-length
mink coat. Late that afternoon, Eddie was on his way home from
his after-school job when he spotted his inebriated father slumped
on a bench in a small neighborhood park. With a great deal of
effort, Eddie managed to get his father home. Since no one else
was home at the time, Eddie put him into bed and phoned the
family physician for further instructions.

The events of that afternoon have been completely repressed
by Eddie's father. He has absolutely no recall of what took place,
and thus his feelings of self-worth are not threatened. However,

Eddie's feeling of self-worth has been reduced by this incident and he would do well to discuss it with his counselor.

Repression should not be confused with *suppression*, which is a conscious act. In repression, our unconscious protects us from feelings of unworthiness by helping us to forget past unpleasantries; thus, repression is not a conscious process and we are unaware that it is taking place. Sometimes when we make a conscious effort to suppress distasteful memories, we find it extremely difficult to do so; occasionally, that which we consciously wish to forget seems all the more tenaciously to cling to our awareness. In suppression, an individual consciously conceals and controls disagreeable desires, experiences, feelings or thoughts. You may be irked at a classmate who has done something grossly unfair to you, and you might like to slap his face, but you suppress this urge and continue on with your other activities.

## OTHER DEFENSE MECHANISMS

*Dissociation* is a defense mechanism in which there is a psychological detachment of the emotional implications from a specific stressful situation. The individual rejects the whole reality, separates it into two parts and, thus, evades the anxiety-provoking condition. It involves the "Yes, but—" approach.

Jimmy's father has been working for many years at a job which he dislikes and which requires much less ability than he possesses. He left college after having completed only one year of study and, at that time, was pleased with the position he obtained. Many times in the ensuing years, friends and relatives provoked him by questioning why he did not resign and seek something more compatible with his capabilities. When thus aroused, he invariably replied, "*Yes, but* I have a family to support."

If Jimmy's father could have faced up to the total reality, he would have seen that because of his family more suitable employment would have been desirable. However, to seek other employment, he needed his wife's encouragement, which he did not receive. To change jobs would have required more courage and more initiative than Jimmy's father possessed; to admit to these shortcomings would have been devastating to his ego and, thus, he said, "Yes, but—." It would have been better for Jimmy's father to have visited the counseling center of his local university, where he would have received the advice and counsel which would have helped him toward a more adequate, realistic resolution of his problem. Had Jimmy's father done this, he would have acquired additional courage, which in turn would have bolstered Jimmy's self-confidence.

*Denial* is an unconscious disavowal of any undesirable deeds, needs, feelings, thoughts or wishes. The specific act or experience which threatens the person's ego-integrity is removed from reality. Frankie's older sister had gotten into difficulties and left school during the middle of last term to live with an aunt in another part of the state. Some of Frankie's classmates made snide insinuations regarding the reason for her leaving. Frankie found the truth intolerable, and this unconscious defensive process came to his rescue. He denied any improper behavior on the part of his older sister; she is "a nice girl who never did anything wrong," he insisted.

*Rationalization* is a mechanism whereby a person tries to justify unbearable behavior, experiences, thoughts or feelings by means of some seemingly reasonable excuse. The person who does this is often said to be "kidding himself." A popular form of rationalization is the *"sour grapes"* aproach, in which an individual insists that he truly does not want a certain something which he did not get (although he truly *does* very much want it).

Nancy eagerly yearned to become the Junior Sugar Maple Queen of her township. When another girl was selected, Nancy loudly proclaimed that she was "the luckiest girl in the world" not to have been chosen, since, she said, it was "such a stupid title" that she would have been "ashamed to carry it" and would have "turned down the title" if it had been awarded to her. Nancy was rationalizing via the "sour grapes" approach.

*"Sweet lemon"* is the reverse of "sour grapes." In this defensive process, the rationalizer accepts the situation in which he finds himself or accepts the thing which he has received because he has no alternative, and although he is inwardly very unhappy about the situation or the thing, he proclaims that this is exactly what he wants.

Another form of rationalization is *blame transference.* The boy who fails the geometry test may say that he was unable to study because the neighbors had a noisy party; the girl who steps on her escort's toes while dancing may blame her new shoes and say they are too tight. Transferring the blame to another person or to some thing helps to reduce the rationalizer's feelings of inferiority. The person or thing upon whom the blame is thrust is known as the *scapegoat.*

*Compensation* is a defensive process whereby a person tries to offset or overcome his real or imagined imperfections. Some people attempt to compensate for their inadequacies by disparaging others. They seek to raise their rank or to elevate their self-esteem by defaming the reputations of those who are superior to them. This is a form of negative, destructive compensation.

Compensation can also be constructive and positive; however, generally such compensation is performed on the conscious level. Under such circumstances, the individual tries to make up for his real or imagined deficiency by putting in its place a wholesome, satisfying substitute. Charlie, who had been a weak, sickly child, was zealously determined to be as strong and hardy as his older brother. He exercised diligently, with his doctor's approval, participated actively in school athletic programs, and has become a star football and baseball player.

*Displacement, identification* and *projection* are other versions of compensation.

*Displacement* is the transfer of an emotion from the original object or person to which it might more naturally be directed to another object or person which serves as an acceptable alternate. *Negative transference* takes place when hostility rather than affection is involved in the transfer.

*Sublimation* also is a type of displacement; it is the deflection of an individual's drives and energies into more socially and personally acceptable pathways. Energies, which might have been exhausted in carrying out consciously unacceptable basic urges, have been channeled positively into such areas as artistic, dramatic, musical and social endeavors.

*Identification* is a compensatory process by which a person strives to lessen his liablities, real or imagined, by allying himself with the assets of another person or group. By identifying with and patterning himself after an accepted person or group, he bolsters his fragile ego and receives a vicarious thrill from the accomplishments of this other person or group. Students identify with their school teams, and when their teams win the individual students experience the glow of victory as though it were a personal triumph. Identification should not be confused with *imitation,* which is a conscious effort to emulate someone whom you admire.

*Projection* is a means of bolstering one's self-esteem by ascribing one's own unacceptable feelings to someone else. However, by projecting his own undesirable thoughts, traits, feelings and wishes on others, a person reveals a great deal about himself. The person who is a habitual liar often judges all others to be liars. He who is greedy may charge those around him with greediness. He who is untrustworthy rarely trusts anyone else. When one woman accuses another of being jealous of her, frequently, the reverse is true; it is the accuser who is generally jealous of the woman she is accusing.

We project not only our negative traits and feelings onto others, but also our positive, desirable ones. Thus, an honest person usually looks upon others as honest too. The thoughtful individual, in the main, regards others as thoughtful. There are specialized psychological examinations, called *projective techniques,* which are so constructed that the person tested responds by projecting his positive and negative feelings, thoughts and traits, and thus divulges considerable information about his basic personality.

All people at some times in their lives use any one or several of these or other versions of defense mechanisms; it is perfectly normal to do so. Their excessive use, however, indicates that the user is not well adjusted and is not seeking more realistic, more satisfactory approaches to solving his stressful situations. To flee from conflict, to make excuses, to behave like infants, to blame others or to disclaim the threatening regions of reality, as we do when we use these unconsciously functioning defense mechanisms, does help to reduce tensions at times of great stress, but it does not solve the problem which triggered the defense mechanism into action. When the problem is not solved and the source of conflict is unresolved, *psychosomatic disorders* often result.

## PSYCHOSOMATIC DISORDERS

Psychic stress frequently has serious effects on physical illness. The word "psychosomatic" comes from the Greek "psyche" (mind) and "soma" (body) and refers to those bodily ailments which are caused or aggravated by emotional disturbances. Essentially, psychosomatic disorders are the product of the pressures resulting from inability to realistically face up to problem situations.

Our emotional reactions have very definite effects, positive and negative, upon the nature of our illnesses and the speed with which we recuperate from these illnesses. Many physicians have told tales of the truly amazing recovery of very ill patients whose deep love of life and zest for living have helped them to overcome serious illness. Similarly, excessive worry, anger, baseless apprehensions and negative attitudes on the part of other patients have hindered their progress and recovery.

Since the functions of the mind and the body are so closely interrelated and interconnected, it could be said that all illnesses have, to a greater or lesser degree, certain psychosomatic aspects. Emotional disturbances, however, seem especially to produce or intensify high blood pressure, headaches, insomnia, cardiac spasms, digestive disturbances, fatigue, ennui, allergies, ulcers, muscular pains and numerous other ailments which come under the broad category of psychosomatic disorders. These same illnesses may sometimes have essentially physical or physiological origins. Headaches, for example, are often basically psychosomatic; yet, headaches may be caused too by respiratory infections, by eating improperly prepared foods, by the presence of brain tumors and by miscellaneous other causes.

Psychosomatic disorders are not the same as *hypochondria*. The hypochondriac is overconcerned with his health and imagines that he is suffering from some specific sickness; however, his symptoms are essentially psychological and there is no organic basis for his complaints. The victim of a psychosomatic disorder truly has a physical illness; something is wrong internally, and unlike the hypochondriac, his is a real, not imaginary, bodily disorder. The hypochondriac exhibits a form of neurotic behavior.

## NEUROTIC BEHAVIOR

A *neurosis* is a behavior disorder resulting from a person's inability to adequately resolve unconscious emotional conflicts. It is a mild disturbance in contrast to the more severe form of behavior disorder, the *psychosis*, which is more popularly known as mental illness.

The neurosis is caused fundamentally by emotional maladjustment; the psychosis is a major mental disturbance whose cause may be organic, chemical, physiological or emotional. The neurotic is unhappy and maladjusted but is able to maintain contact with the real world, whereas the psychotic has lost much of his contact with reality and may suffer from such distortions as *delusions* (irrational beliefs and thoughts, such as baselessly thinking someone wishes to harm him) and *hallucinations* (false sensory perceptions resulting in seeing people or things which are not actually there).

*Illusions* are sometimes confused with delusions and hallucinations, but they are entirely different. Illusions are perfectly normal misinterpretations of sensory experiences. Thus, when you are on a moving train, you often get the impression that the houses, trees and other parts of the scenery are moving and that your train is standing still; this is an illusion, for you are misinterpreting what you are actually seeing. Similarly, short women wear dresses with vertical stripes to create the illusion that they are taller, and automobile manufacturers place horizontal metal strips along the sides of cars to give the illusion of greater car length.

Basically, the neurotic is unable to adjust realistically to stressful or lesser situations. He is often troubled by feelings of inferiority and guilt. The defense mechanisms which he employed failed to function adequately and did not reduce his tensions. As his anxieties increased, neurotic symptoms appeared. There are varied forms of neuroses, just as there are of the psychoses, and they may range from rather mild to more aggravated emotional ailments.

Neurotic behavior may include simple, but nondisabling constant complaints of persistent fatigue and feelings of uneasiness and being below par when there are no physiological or external causes for these. Some neurotics experience irrational fears, known as *phobias* (see Chapter 6, section "Facing Up to Fears"), which may restrict or cause alterations in their daily activities.

*Obsessions* and *compulsions* are more incapacitating forms of neurotic behavior. Obsessions are tenacious thoughts which keep recurring although they are unwanted. Compulsions are similarly tenacious, recurring and unwanted, but in contrast to obsessive thoughts, these involve urges to perform certain acts. Neurotics who suffer from the type of neurosis known as *obsessive-compulsive reaction* may, for example, be troubled by silly or unpleasant thoughts or feel compelled to repeatedly, unnecessarily wash their hands or touch every post or walk along every crack in the pavement or count from one to ten each time they see a midget; the hypochondriac suffers from this type of neurosis.

The neurotic's inability to cope adequately with his anxieties hampers his life and makes him unable to achieve as much as he otherwise might. It is important at an early age to learn to confront problems realistically rather than to repeatedly run away from them or to use any other defense mechanisms. Facing up to problems and learning from our failures strengthens our character and gives us greater ability to contend with and conquer future problems.

How can you best consciously confront and constructively combat the complex conflicts of life? Let us consider the ways whereby this can be accomplished.

# 8

# PROBLEMS ARE WHAT PEOPLE HAVE

MANY PEOPLE, WHEN THEY ENCOUNTER AN ES-
pecially vexing problem, tend to say, "Oh, why does this happen
only to me!"

Well, it does not happen only to you or only to anyone else.
It happens to all of us. If it is any consolation to you, remember,
when you have an especially burdensome problem, that at that
same moment there are millions of people who are also facing
oppressive personal problems. No, they are not facing the exact
same problem that you are—although, in many cases, there may
be great similarities—but their problems are as burdensome to
them as yours is to you.

Everywhere, there are people with problems.

## PROBLEMS, PROBLEMS, PROBLEMS

Problems, like the palliative pills which are taken to ease
them, come in all sizes, shapes and shades. There are ever so
many kinds of problems—career, family, financial, health, marital, personal, religious, school, social and a variety of others;

then, too, within each of these areas, there are countless specific individual problems.

What is a "problem"? Basically, a problem is a situation which results when a barrier prevents you from achieving your aim; your aim may be to reach a particular goal or to maintain a satisfying situation or to achieve or receive whatever it is that you may desire.

A problem may be "big" or "small," depending upon whose problem it is, who is judging its magnitude, and the perspective of the judger. All too often, people tend to regard other people's big problems as small and their own small problems as big. Also, problems which were very important to you yesterday may appear insignificant today; unfortunately, sometimes yesterday's seemingly insignificant problem may become today's major problem.

How you react to your problems, big or small, depends essentially upon your personality and the nature and intensity of the problem. Your reaction to the problem depends too upon the nature of the barrier in your path. Sometimes the barrier may be very concrete; other times, it may be quite intangible. Thus, you may be on your way to an important appointment and suddenly find yourself caught in a traffic jam. The barrier is the very concrete backlog of cars, and your problem is how to get to your appointment as promptly as possible despite these cars.

Then, you may be faced with a problem of a totally different nature. You may be very pleased about having been accepted for admission into a certain well-known, highly regarded college, when you discover that a classmate is spreading vicious lies, saying that your father paid money to an unnamed college official to gain your admission. Here, the barrier is this intangible slanderous threat to your continued good reputation, and your problem is how to withstand and counteract this attack.

Numerous commonplace problems of lesser severity than the aforementioned face you each day. Perhaps this morning you were faced with the problem of which sweater you should wear. It was cold outside and you wanted to wear something which would both keep you warm and help you to look attractive.

Depending upon your personality, you may have reacted to this problem in a variety of ways within the range of the following responses: (1) you snatched the first sweater in your closet and slipped into it, (2) you glanced through the closet, considered several possibilities and then made a thoughtful selection or (3) you carefully examined every garment in your closet, then pondered and pondered as though this was the weightiest of problems and, finally, made a hasty decision when the clock indicated that you were late for your first class.

Just as simple problems are quite serious for some people, others with relatively weighty problems are unperturbed.

Because you have a problem does not mean that you are a problem. All people have problems. Not all people are problems. What differentiates people from one another is not so much the nature of their problems, but how they approach their problems.

## APPROACHES TO PROBLEMS

Considering the nature of YOUR personality and the nature of YOUR problems, how can YOU consciously confront, counteract and conquer these problems?

There is a wide range of basic, conscious approaches to problems. Thus, when a young person is faced with a perplexing problem, he may react in any one or several of the following ways or varied versions of them:

1. Run away from the problem (this is the same action as that which occurs in the escape mechanism, but here the person is conscious of what he is doing).

2. Shout or cry in anger at the barrier in his pathway, but do nothing about it.

3. Quietly sit and wonder why that has happened to him, but do nothing in the hope that it will go away.

4. Worry and worry and worry, but take no action against it.

5. Conclude that the situation is hopeless, consider his aim a "lost cause" and decide to "give up" and "suffer the consequences."

6. Judge the barrier to be impenetrable and alter his course.

7. Attempt to go around the barrier, hoping that perhaps the barrier thereby may be circumvented and his aim might yet be achieved.

8. Delve right into the barrier with a come-what-may attitude.

9. Think the problem through as rationally as possible and decide upon the specific attack which might be best for this specific problem.

10. Work on the problem persistently and patiently, giving it all the thought and time it requires; then, as needed, consult with parents, school counselor or psychologist, family physician, clergyman or other knowledgeable adult and with the aid of this consultation, make his own best judgment on how to overcome that barrier in his pathway.

11. Get away for a short period of relaxation, return with renewed perspective and vigor, and then apply No. 10 above.

Which one of these approaches or which combination of them you use to face your problems will vary with the kind of person you are and the kinds of problems confronting you. The greater the emotional content of the individual problem, the more involved you will become with the problem and the greater too will be the intensity of the involvement.

## CAN YOU TAKE IT?

When a problem defies solution or is exceedingly difficult to solve, the person confronted by it may become frustrated. When you are frustrated in your aims, are you ready to "give up" or do you persist in fighting on?

Some people are capable of enduring many major problems; they may be thwarted time after time, and yet they persist until they reach their goal. These are the people who have a high frustration tolerance. In simple language, it is said that they can "take it." Other people surrender to comparatively minor problems; they cannot bear any blockage in the satisfaction of their needs or desires. These are the people with low frustration tolerance.

Which kind of person are you? Are you the kind who can take it? A great deal depends upon your outlook on life and your self-esteem. Generally, the person with an optimistic outlook can take a great deal more frustration than the pessimist can; often, the presence of a barrier presents a challenge, causing the optimist and the person with wholesome self-esteem to fight even harder and to persist with even greater tenacity in order to reach a desired goal. The pessimist has many self-doubts and is, therefore, ready to give up more quickly. As you noted at the meeting of the Tender Ten, Dolores, the pessimist, had little hope for the success of the project and wanted to make no further attempts to salvage the wreckage after the ill-fated gathering.

Some people take the attitude that if they sit and wait and let time pass, their problems will solve themselves. They have developed a way of living patiently with their frustrations. It is true that time is often a healer. There are some problems which somehow do dissolve with the passage of time. In some instances, a problem may actually be solved by time's passage; in others, the problem remains unresolved, but from today's perspective yesterday's problem may appear to be of lesser importance. Oftentimes, however, yesterday's problem, if not approached and attacked in a realistic, rational fashion, may grow greater and be an even more serious problem today.

There are unfortunately some problems which defy solution, and the people troubled by them must learn to live with and accept these situations as best they can. A famous little poem, used as an inspirational guide by many, goes as follow:

> "God give me the serenity to accept the things I
>     cannot change,
> The courage to change the things I can,
> And the wisdom to know the difference."

## YOUNG PEOPLE'S PROBLEMS

People of all age levels generally want to belong, to be needed, to be admired, to be respected; to the young person, these wants are especially strong, and if they are not met in a wholesome manner, problems arise. The problems which loom largest among young people are those which center around the subject of popularity and their relationships with their peers. Since the subject of popularity is such a major one, the next chapter is devoted entirely to it.

Young people have numerous additional problems especially related to their age level. You also have your individual personal problems. In the main, however, most of these problems have a great deal in common with the problems of your contemporaries. Although it may not ease your personal pain to know that others are suffering for similar reasons, it may be comforting to discover that you were not alone in being singled out to suffer. Because of this, young people are often aided by group discussions of their problems.

A popular group technique for helping young people with their problems is the socio-guidrama. The socio-guidrama series contains a number of playlets each of which dramatically highlights a specific problem of young people. Each socio-guidrama takes about eight or ten minutes to present. These playlets are acted out by the students themselves in the assemblies or class-

rooms in thousands of junior and senior high schools in the
United States and Canada. They are also used in churches and
synagogues at youth fellowship meetings, in community centers
and miscellaneous youth gatherings, and at P.T.A. meetings
where the parents often do the acting.

Socio-guidramas present real-life problems which confront
young people. They do not, however, answer these problems,
because there are no pat answers to people's problems. You and
your best friend may have what appear to be identical problems.
However, the best possible solution to your problem may differ
radically from the best possible solution to your friend's problem. There are many reasons for this. You are both entirely
different people with different personalities, different needs, different home situations, different parents, different potentials,
and so on and on with a vast number of differences which call
for a solution to your problem quite unlike your best friend's
solution.

Although these playlets do not present you with pretty platters
of answers to your problems, for there are no such pretty
platters in life, they do stimulate you and your classmates to
discuss the problems which face you. This wholesome discussion and realistic interplay of thoughts between you and your
classmates help you and them to understand yourselves and your
problems all the better. This aids you in finding the most satisfactory solutions to your specific problem situations.

The playlets cover such problem areas as ambition, career
choice, cheating, college and scholarships, dating, delinquency,
drinking, driving, family relations, friendship, going steady, job
interviews, marriage, parent-child relations, prejudice, self-confidence, smoking and television viewing. Further information
about these playlets may be obtained from their publisher,
Methods and Materials Press, 6 South Derby Road, Springfield,
New Jersey 07081. (A list of titles may be found in the appendix
of this book.)

You and your friends are going through a time of much inner

change and development. Like most of your contemporaries, you probably want to assert your independence, yet you would like to hold on to the comforts which come from your dependence on your parents. In the midst of this ambivalence is found one of the most common problems of young people, namely, the prevalent bemoaning of the fact that their parents do not trust them. This absence of trust is found in many areas of young people's experiences.

There are parents who do not trust their children in their choice of friends, in their behavior on dates, in their career and college choices, in the spending of their allowances and in many other matters. If this is true in your home too, make an effort to sit down with your parents and discuss your specific problem with them. In your own mind, review your recent behavior as it pertains to your problem situation. Try to be objective about it—admittedly, this is difficult—and ask yourself, "Have I been behaving in a manner which makes it difficult for my parents to trust me?"

If your answer to this question is "Yes," then concentrate on modifying your behavior to make you deserving of your parents' trust. Nancy was especially peeved by the fact that her father refused to trust her with substantial sums of money for the purchase of large items. Her father insisted that Nancy could not manage money properly.

## MANY MISMANAGE MONEY

Not only Nancy and some of her friends, but many adults too mismanage money. Money, however, is a special problem to young people. Millions of teen-agers throughout the country work after school hours, on Saturdays and/or during their summer vacation. For many, this earned income supplements the allowances which they receive from their parents. For others, this income may be sufficient to replace the allowance. In either case, the money they earn gives young people a sense of independence. It also gives them a sense of power. They are able to buy and to do many of the things which they otherwise could not.

Whether the money you possess comes entirely from your allowance or is a combination of allowance and earned income or is entirely earned income, this money gives you the opportunity to show your parents how trustworthy and how sensible you are. Money is for using, but it is important to use it wisely. This use takes three forms: (1) spending, (2) sharing and (3) saving.

A major portion of your weekly income you spend on yourself for items needed in your daily school and social activities. A second portion should go to helping those who are less fortunate than you. Emotionally healthy people possess the feeling of love for their fellow human beings and are capable of sharing some of their money (and their time and efforts) with worthwhile charities to aid those in need. The third portion of your money should be saved for a later date. Your original savings plus the accumulated interest will help you in the future toward paying for specialized training in college or technical school or for some other important purpose.

With money, as with most other matters in life, moderation is recommended. Some people hoard their money and begrudge themselves not only certain luxuries which they can afford but even some basic necessities. These are often people who feel unloved and rejected. The money they hold onto so tightly is a replacement for the love they have not received or are not now receiving. Conversely, there are insecure people lacking in a feeling of self-worth, who believe they can bolster their sense of security by being "big spenders." They are forever trying "to keep up with the Joneses," although they are financially unable to do so. Such a person is Nancy's mother.

Nancy's mother yearned for a mink coat. She pressured her husband to work harder and to earn more money so she could afford to make this purchase. Recently, she bought a full-length mink coat by paying one-third down and the remainder in twenty-four monthly payments. For many years, Nancy's mother had prodded her husband and insisted that when she got a mink coat, from that day forward, she would never again feel socially unacceptable. After getting her mink coat, she made a noteworthy discovery—she felt as insecure and as socially unacceptable as ever!

This is a discovery made by many women who buy expensive fur coats for reasons other than to keep them warm in the winter. A mink coat—or any other item—does not, of itself, make anyone socially acceptable or unacceptable. You must accept yourself before you can feel socially acceptable. The feeling of self-worth, of acceptability, resides within you. It is internal and not something external that you can put on and take off at will like a fancy garment.

Nancy's mother learned, as many others like her have, that her mink coat made little or no impression on those she was seeking to impress and that it did impress (and this was often a negative impression resulting in envy) those whom she did not care to impress. Thus, she found herself again plagued by her old feelings of inadequacy and inferiority. Nancy's mother has many positive, socially acceptable qualities. She is basically a kind, compassionate and competent woman. However, all too often, she keeps these qualities locked within herself due to her sense of false values and her desire for luxuries beyond her financial reach.

She could bring her good qualities out into public view by performing more frequent acts of kindness to others, by offering some of her free time as a volunteer aide in a hospital or similar institution, and by doing a good job at her work, thus making her competency evident. This behavior would build her inner feeling of self-worth, and the recognition she would receive from others because of her involvement in worthwhile, meaningful activities would strengthen her self-confidence. Her need to seek attention and acceptance by squandering money on unnecessary material items would then be reduced, and the family finances could be more properly used for more valuable purposes.

Nancy similarly suffers from feelings of inadequacy and social insecurity, and therefore uses her allowance on expensive clothing in hopes these will make her more socially accepted. Her father points to garments in her closet which she bought to impress a friend and wore only once or never at all. Nancy admits that this is so, but nonetheless is angered by her father's unwillingness to trust her.

As with her mother, Nancy should utilize her potential and her positive attributes to a greater extent so she would receive more recognition for the talents and capabilities she possesses. She and her parents should also have a discussion on the fundamentals of budgeting.

To manage your money more wisely, draw a line down the center of a blank piece of paper and write the word "Income" at the head of the left-hand column and the word "Expenditures" at the head of the right-hand column. In the "Income" column, list the amount of your weekly allowance plus any earnings or other sources of income which you may have.

In the "Expenditures" column, list your varied expenses, remembering to consider spending, saving and sharing. In the first category, include such items as school expenses, club dues, recreational costs, items of apparel, grooming and beauty preparations and needs, magazines and hobby items. You should make every effort to save approximately ten per cent of your income for some special worthy future purpose, and an appropriate amount should be set aside for donation to deserving charities.

If your "Expenditures" column exceeds your "Income" column, you have an unbalanced budget. You are faced with the choice of either reducing your expenditures or increasing your income. Review the items in your "Expenditures" column. Are there any items which are rather unnecessary and could just as well be eliminated? If not, or if there are some but your expenditures are still too high, perhaps you can increase your income by earning some money working at some part-time after-school activity. If you show your parents that you can be trusted with money, perhaps they will consider increasing your allowance.

In all matters, as with money management, if you wish to be trusted by your parents and by others, you should behave in a manner which demonstrates that you merit their trust. Nancy would earn her father's trust if she would show him that she could live within her budget and could manage her money in a more mature manner. Nancy mismanages money in her quest for attention and acceptance. Cathy's desire for acceptance and approval brought her face to face with another problem prevalent among young people, namely, the problem of cheating.

## CHEATING IS SELF-DEFEATING

Cathy's brother, excessively indulged by his aunt and pampered by his parents, constantly insulted and bullied Cathy. Her obesity problem stemmed in part from this unhappy sibling situation. Her yearning for some of the attention and approval which was being heaped upon her brother drove her one day to cheating on a chemistry test.

Cathy had decided to take the chemistry course because one of her close friends was doing so (not at all a good reason for taking any course!) and because she thought she might need it for admission to the college she hoped someday to attend. She had difficulties with the subject matter from the very start of the term.

When her chemistry teacher announced the first test, Cathy was tempted to go to the school counselor to discuss her problem with him. At the last moment, she changed her mind and decided to take the test instead. During the examination period, it became obvious to Cathy that she did not have enough knowledge of the subject to pass. She was so afraid that her brother would poke fun at her if she failed that, for the first time in her life, she resorted to cheating.

Cathy was not caught cheating by her teacher, but she was reproached by her own conscience. The day after the test, she visited her school counselor, confessed about her cheating and told him why. The counselor worked with her, revised her program and helped her to develop positive insights, greater understanding and more tolerance of her home situation. With his assistance, she has become involved in worthwhile extra-curricular activities to raise her self-esteem and has taken other constructive steps to reduce the possibility of ever again finding it necessary to cheat.

People who cheat are often emotionally impoverished. They lack sufficient feeling of self-acceptance and self-worth. The actual cheating, however, defeats the cheater and his purpose. The higher mark the student may obtain as a result of cheating (if he is not caught!) does not elevate his feeling of self-worth; as a matter of fact, it diminishes his self-esteem, for he knows that this higher mark was not honestly gotten. High school and college students have indicated on many occasions that they consider cheating to be morally wrong.

Establish good study habits—and even more important, strengthen your set of moral values—and you will be far less likely to succumb to academic (or other) dishonesty. If you continue to have difficulties with certain subjects, make an appointment to see your school counselor and discuss your problem with him. Keep your standards of academic integrity and moral behavior high. Deviating from these standards will reduce your personal acceptance of yourself and intensify your original problem. A form of conduct closely related to cheating is lying.

## LIES—THE SIMPLE, SELF-SERVING AND SLANDEROUS KINDS

Rare indeed is the person who has not at some time lied. The simple and self-serving lies are the rather harmless ones by which, for example, a girl may say she purchased her dress at an exclusive shoppe when actually she bought it in a bargain basement or by which a boy may say he went out with "a gorgeous, glamorous blonde" when in truth he dated the homely girl who lives down the block.

These lies enable the persons who do the lying to save face, to bolster their sagging egos and to feel temporarily somewhat more important than they usually feel. If the practice persists and the person becomes a chronic liar, then the condition is potentially quite harmful. The chronic liar does so because there are situations in his real world which he considers unpleasant and unacceptable to him. Through his lies, he verbally (but not really) temporarily transforms these into pleasant, acceptable situations. Generally, however, when the liar thinks he has fooled others, he has only fooled himself.

The chronic liar needs professional help to determine the underlying cause (or causes) of his chronic lying. Perhaps his views of his real world are distorted because of a false sense of values; perhaps his world is truly not as unpleasant as he views it; or perhaps he is refusing to face a reality which simply must be faced.

Lying is the conscious version of denial, the defense mechanism which operates on an unconscious level (Chapter 7). It serves only as a temporary tension-reducer, but does not alter the problem situation which is disturbing the person who is lying. The chronic liar needs guidance to assess the situation more realistically and to cope with it more adequately and more wholesomely.

Slander is the harmful, heinous kind of lie. The slanderer spreads falsehoods about someone whom he wants to injure. Jimmy received a notification of acceptance by the first college of his choice. His high school record is a splendid one; his academic average is high; his extracurricular record is very good; he did exceptionally well on the College Board examinations; and his teachers, counselor and principal have recommended him highly for college admission. Thus, Jimmy was readily accepted by a noted Ivy League school. Another boy, a classmate of Jimmy's, applied to the same college and was summarily rejected. This boy then spread the slander that Jimmy was accepted because his father had bribed one of the officers on the college's admissions staff.

When this slander came to Jimmy's attention, he became incensed. He could not very well extract from the air the vicious words which his classmate had said about him. He visited his school counselor and learned from him that slanderers generally say about their victims what is true of themselves. Thus, it was true that his classmate's father had attempted to bribe a college official in order to gain his son's admission, but the bribe was refused. This boy's record was below par and so he was not accepted.

It was a consolation for Jimmy to learn—and it may similarly console others who have suffered or may someday suffer from the slings of slander—that the more you achieve and stand out from the crowd, the more you arouse the jealousies of the unhappy, frustrated nonachievers, and thus the more likely you are to be slandered by these unhappy people. Slanderers are troubled, discontented people, and they describe themselves by the lies they spread about their victims.

When a woman spreads lies about other women's husbands, saying that these men are misbehaving, it often indicates that her husband is misbehaving (or that she is afraid he is). When a man says that all of his business associates are dishonest, it generally means that he is dishonest in his business transactions. The person who trusts nobody is himself not to be trusted.

When Jimmy's equanimity was restored as a result of having spoken with his counselor, he was capable of compassion for the classmate who had slandered him. Jimmy's problem was how to cope with the slanderous attack on his integrity; by discussing it with his counselor, he approached and conquered it acceptably and wholesomely. His slanderer has a problem and is a problem; this boy is under great pressure from his parents to go to college, although he does not want to go and is not qualified. To alleviate his problem, he and his parents need assistance and should make an appointment to speak with the school counselor.

As a direct contrast to the slanderous lie which aims to deceive, there is the "white lie" which aims to relieve. Some may question why anyone should use any form of lies at all.

## THE "WHY'S" OF WHITE LIES

The white lie, in a way, is a type of tactful talk diplomatically designed to soothe the feelings of the person at whom it is directed. Whereas slander accuses and abuses, the white lie eases and appeases.

Do you want to hurt a friend's feelings? Do you enjoy telling someone you think he is a bore? Do you like to inform a neighbor that she has no ability? Well, there are countless occasions when it is kinder to apply the white lie than to tell the truth.

Let us say that you are attending a party and you are utterly bored by all who are present. Should you tell your host and hostess that you consider their guests dull and are, therefore, leaving? Or should you feign illness, say you have a headache and consequently must leave? Let us say too that you have a nice neighbor who loves to bake pies, but is a dreadful cook. The next time you visit her and she offers you a piece of her freshly baked pie, should you refuse and tell her the truth about the stomach-ache you had when you ate one of her previous pies? Or should you say you are on a diet and must not partake of any pies?

Yes, there are situations, such as these, when the truth is unkind and may be socially disastrous and when using the little white lie is the wise and tactful thing to do. Tactful talk and thoughtful behavior will help to make you a more positively popular person.

# 9
# THE POSITIVELY POPULAR YOU

WHEN YOUNG PEOPLE ARE ASKED WHAT IS THEIR
most pressing problem, the most frequent reply revolves around
the question, "How can I be popular?"

Like most young people—and most older folks too—you want
to be liked, to be admired, to belong. You want to have friends
and to be an accepted member of a group. Essentially, you are
in search of popularity.

Exactly what is this popularity which you and your contemporaries are seeking?

## POPULARITY—POSITIVE AND NEGATIVE

According to Webster's dictionary, "popularity" means "the
quality or state of being popular, the manifest approval or esteem
of many persons or of people in general"; and "popular" means
"commonly liked or found pleasant or praiseworthy." These are
good basic definitions. Now, let us go beyond the basics into
the different types of popularity.

Yes, you want approval; you want to be liked. But by whom?
By what kinds of people? There are both positive and negative
types of popularity, and there is a big difference between these
two. Those who are positively popular are liked by the right

kind of people for the right reasons. Those who are negatively popular are liked by the wrong people for unwholesome, improper reasons. Thus, the girl who indicates by her behavior that boys can go as far as they wish with her will become popular—negatively popular, that is. Her popularity will be based on being liked by boys of low standards who are attracted to her for lustful reasons.

The desire to be popular is so very strong among young people that some are ready to settle for negative popularity just as long as they are popular and feel as though they belong to some group. This may lead them into associations with the wrong group, with so-called bad company. This need not and should not happen to you—and you can prevent it from happening. Those who get involved with "bad company" do so in an attempt to revolt against authority. They try through this immature approach to assert their independence. Basically, these young people have very little feeling of self-worth and very low opinions of themselves and, therefore, believe that "good company" would not want them.

Well, you can be assured that "good company" will want you, if you make yourself "wantable." If you want people to like you, you must make yourself likable. When a group of young people were asked what it was that they liked about certain people, they replied that they like those who are cooperative, unselfish, considerate, well-mannered and interested in others.

Ask yourself what kind of people you like. Probably, you will reply as most people do, by saying that you are attracted to those who say nice things to you, who are kind to you, who show consideration and concern for you.

All right then, if you like others to say nice things to you, don't you think that others would like you to say nice things to them? Well, then, why don't you say such things? And, don't just mouth words you don't mean; mean them! There is no place here for lying, not even for the little white lies. Don't be a hypocrite!

Intelligent people will readily recognize and resent hypocrisy, and rightfully so. Speak truthfully. There certainly must be something nice you can say about people you meet and know, people with whom you would like to become friends; if there were nothing nice about them, you wouldn't want to become friends with them, would you?

At a class party, several girls admired the new dress worn by one of their classmates, and they told her how well she looked in it. Susie later approached this same girl and said, "That dress looks terrible on you. It makes you look like an old lady."

There is no excuse for such unkindness. If your opinion is not asked, don't give it. If it is asked, then make every effort to say something positive and pleasant. Let us say your girl friend asks you whether you think her new hat is becoming to her. Perhaps you don't like the style, but, remember, you are not a millinery expert. Think a moment. Isn't the color cheerfully bright? Then, say so. Aren't the flowers on it attractive? Then, say so. Isn't the shape of it suitable for her face? Then, say that too. Look for the acceptable and agreeable—and yet truthful—things you can say and then say them.

Ask yourself if you like people who are thoughtless. You don't, do you? Well, then, why should people like you if you are thoughtless of them? Do you like those who must always have their way? No? Well, then, why should they like you if you insist on always having things your way? Do you like people who show no gratitude for gifts given to them or kindnesses shown to them? No? Well, then, why should people think well of you if you are ungrateful to them?

If the negative adjectives are descriptive of your behavior, you should and can make efforts to change, and you should start right now! There are those who say they cannot change; they cannot because they don't want to change! By saying they cannot change, they are offering to themselves and to the public what, to them, seems like a good excuse for not changing; it offers them an easy way out. You can change for the better if you want to do so; it is not easy, but it can be done and it is worth doing.

We can all be more thoughtful, more cooperative, more mannerly, more considerate, more generous, more unselfish, more interested in others and more grateful than we are. We all have our human failings, but we can all be better and do better—and we should all try. It is well worth the effort. Make that effort. It will help make you a more positively popular person. Your popularity then will be based on your being a sensible, constructive citizen and on being liked by other similarly sensible people. It will not be the negative kind of popularity based on immature or immoral behavior or on your acting like some darn fool at whom others may laugh or scoff when you turn your back.

Positive character traits developed and strengthened at home and at school today will help you to have pleasanter relationships in the outside world tomorrow. Start now to practice positive personality patterns in your relations with your relatives and your classmates. Be thoughtful and tactful in your talk and action. Remember, words can wound, so use care in what you say. Think—before you speak. Think—before you act. Show consideration for the feelings of others.

To enhance your popularity, listen to people when they speak to you. You do like people to pay attention to you, don't you? Then, listen to them. How much you learn in school and out of school depends on how much and how well you listen. When someone else is speaking, do give him the courtesy of not interrupting. Wait until he is finished and then you will have your turn.

When you do speak, your listeners hear not only what you say, but how you say it. Is your speech too harsh, high or hurried? Try to speak clearly, distinctly and in a well-modulated, properly pitched, unhurried voice. Your speech may attract people to you or repel them from you. If your school's English or speech department has a tape recorder, get permission to use it; it will help you to become aware of any speech defects you may have and help you to correct them and improve your speech.

Yes, you can be positively popular! The most important, most new-fashioned rule for positive popularity in the latter 1960s is the old-fashioned "Golden Rule": Do unto others as you would have others do unto you.

Don't expect—nor should you want—to be popular with everyone you meet. There are some people you will meet whom you will not like and who may not like you. Make friends with those whose aims and standards and ideals are like yours. Put into practice your positive personality traits—and join those school clubs which concern themselves with matters of interest to you. Participate in the youth fellowship activities of your local church or synagogue. Become a member of the young people's groups in your community center.

Don't just join and sit back passively. Take an active part in the proceedings. You will have far more fun if you do. You will be involved in important activities including service to people who need your help. Immerse yourself in these activities, and challenge, inspiration and gratification will be yours—plus, positive popularity based on worthwhile, wholesome friendships.

## FRIENDS AND/OR ACQUAINTANCES

A television performer, not so long ago, stated on the air that he had "millions of friends." This comment brought an abundance of mail to the station and to newspapers and magazines stating that he had misused the word "friend." The listeners were quite correct, for no one has millions of "friends." The performer perhaps had an audience of millions. But millions of friends? No.

Who exactly is a friend? A friend is someone who will come to your aid when you are in need, who will help you up when you are down, who will offer you strength when you are weak.

Some may say that this definition describes a "true friend." But no, the expression "true friend" is a redundancy. Your *friend* is *true*. The only kind of friendship is the true kind; if it is not true, it is not friendship. The term "false friend" is an incongruity. If a person is your friend, he cannot be false; if he is false, he is not your friend.

How many friends have you? We are, with rare exceptions, very fortunate from the moment we enter this world to have two good friends, a mother and a father. Some also have grandparents who are friends. Siblings, aunts, uncles and cousins should be your friends too; realistically—and unfortunately—however, this is not always so. Beyond this point, we must earn our friends. You must be a friend to have a friend.

A friend is a priceless, precious possession. Ask yourself this question: How many people would come to my assistance if I were in trouble, in need, injured or ill? Your reply indicates the number of friends you have—or think you have. A famous movie actress recently told of how she had thought she had a great many friends. Then, one day, she became ill and had to be hospitalized for a rather lengthy period of time. She was shocked, she said, that only two people came to visit her during her period of hospitalization. She learned the hard way that a friend is one who stands by you in times of adversity. Although she was a celebrated actress, she was neither shrewd nor wise enough in the ways of the world to have learned how to differentiate between friends and those who surround a celebrity (or anyone else) for whatever it is they hope to gain thereby.

Friends cannot be bought. Your friend comes to your rescue without thought of reward. The person whose services you buy when you are in need is a "paid worker," not a "friend." (It should be noted, however, that there are instances where a "paid worker"—an employee—may sincerely venerate an employer worthy of such veneration and may indeed be a friend to this employer.)

Make determined efforts not to be unkind or thoughtless or

inconsiderate to anyone. But never ever be unkind or thoughtless toward a friend! It is a most ungrateful way to act, and it is foolish of you to do so, for you do not have that many friends to spare. No one has. If you behaved this way because you were upset by some sad circumstances, apologize for your improper, ungentlemanly (or unladylike) behavior as quickly as possible. Your friend will understand and forgive you.

All too often people confuse the terms "friend" and "acquaintance." They say they have "a great many friends" when they truly mean "a great many acquaintances." We go through life making numerous acquaintances, and these relationships are pleasant but not lasting; friendships, however, are earned and are based on a solid foundation of devotion, admiration and respect.

Some think friendship is based on the length of time two people know each other. This is not necessarily so. You may know one person for a good number of years and yet not have progressed beyond the level of acquaintanceship; whereas you may know a second person for a relatively short period of time, and a strong bond of friendship may have become established between you and this second person. This friendship develops out of mutually high regard and respect for each other.

Our contemporary civilization has made us increasingly dependent upon each other. Young people—and older ones too—strive to reduce the distances between themselves and others. In the rapid pace of our complex societies, individual relationships are often rather superficial. You can increase your friendships and make your relationships more meaningful.

You can have a greater number of friends. Remember, a friend is one who is devoted to you, admires and respects you, and would readily come to your rescue if such rescue were required. But, remember too, you must earn this devotion by behaving in a manner which shows that you are devoted to your friend. You must deserve this respect by giving respect to your friend and to others.

Some people are unable to give respect, for they have little or no self-respect. If you don't give respect to others, you will neither earn nor receive respect from them. If you don't have any respect for yourself, neither will anyone else. You must have feelings of self-worth and wholesome, humble pride to have respect for yourself as an individual. These plus the ability realistically to view and vanquish your problems without blaming others for them form the foundations for your self-respect.

Self-respect is important in all human relationships, but it is especially so in the relationships between members of opposite sexes.

## RATING AT DATING

The teen years are a period of tension and turmoil, of conflict and change. In the midst of this dynamic period, the teen-ager must adjust to his own numerous personal, physical and physiological changes. His bodily structure is growing at what may seem to him and those around him a rather alarming pace. Alterations are taking place within his body systems and organs. His glands are functioning more actively. He is becoming aroused sexually and may, at times, find these sensations and urges disturbing to understand and handle. Faced with new internal and external experiences, the young person must adapt himself to them as best he can.

Wholesome friendships with classmates and others of your age group will help you to facilitate these adjustments, to diminish the self-consciousness and to ease the awkwardness which trouble so many of your contemporaries—and may be troubling you too. Rating at dating is a matter of special concern at this time. What to say and how to behave on a date pose problems for so many young people (often even for those who pretend to be sophisticated). If these are problems to you too, it may comfort you to know that they are not yours alone.

Lost between her mother's desire for material things and her father's preoccupation with her younger brother, Nancy was unable to accept herself as a human being of any worth. She was delighted when Frankie asked her for a first date, so delighted that she did not mind some of his crass comments and boorish behavior. When he told her that he could not afford to take her to the large movie theatre which she wished to attend, she volunteered to buy the tickets. It was soon obvious to Frankie that he could vent his pent-up anger at Nancy without any protest from her. Thus, he continued to use her as his "emotional punching bag" on whom he could release the feelings of rejection and resentment which often welled up within him due to his hostile home situation.

Girls should not suggest going to places where their escorts cannot afford to take them. If the girl likes the boy and he is a suitable date for her, she should be pleased to have a "coke" with him at the local soda fountain; if she doesn't like him and he is unsuitable for her, going to the Super Swank Sweet Shoppe will not make him any more suitable.

Offering to pay his bill only makes matters worse. It indicates that the girl has little if any respect for the boy or for herself. (This is not the same as the "Dutch treat," where neither the boy nor the girl has much money and each pays his own way; this is reasonable, especially among the early teen-agers and particularly if it is not overdone.) The girl belittles the boy when she offers to pay for him, and if he is the right kind of person, he will resent and reject the offer. If he has no self-respect and is not offended by the offer, he is not worth dating. Once this type of boy starts accepting a girl's money, he will continue this practice, just as Frankie has done with Nancy.

Nancy thinks she is Frankie's only "steady," but he is also dating a girl who attends a school in a neighboring community. Since Nancy has no respect for herself, she gets no respect from Frankie. When Frankie no longer needs Nancy as an outlet for his hostilities, he will drop her and truly go steady with the second girl, who does not pay any of his bills and thereby makes Frankie feel more manly.

In psychological terminology, Nancy is known as a masochist.

A masochist is a person who derives pleasure, generally of a sexual nature, from pain inflicted upon her (or him) by herself (or himself) or by someone else. Frankie is a sadist. A sadist is one who gets pleasure, similarly generally of a sexual nature, from inflicting pain on others. In both masochism and sadism, the pain received and the pain inflicted may be either physical or psychological. Sometimes, the masochist may be a sadist too; thus, some masochists enjoy imposing pain upon themselves and then derive pleasure from this self-inflicted pain.

### WAS FATE AT FAULT?

Teen-agers often become indignant when their parents make them toe the mark about whom they date, where they go on a date, how late they stay out and how they behave. Your parents set up rules of conduct for you because they are truly and deeply concerned about you, because they care what happens to you. This is their way of trying to protect you. At this stage in your life, you may think you know more than your parents do. Perhaps, you think they are quite "old-fashioned." Well, be assured that no matter how much you know—or think you know—your parents know more than you do, at least just by virtue of having been around longer than you have. As a matter of fact, the more you actually know and the brighter you are, the more aware you are that your parents know more than you do! So, be kind to yourself, listen to your parents and take heed!

Dolores' older sister, who was eighteen and working as a typist, announced to her parents last summer that she had made a reservation to spend a one-week vacation at a certain resort. Her parents requested that she cancel her reservation, since they had heard reports that this resort attracted a "fast crowd" and they did not consider it a proper place for their daughter. Dolores' sister adamantly refused to accede to her parents' request and did as she pleased. At this resort, she met a tall young man with the physique of a football hero, and she immediately became infatuated with him. She was too inexperienced and too young to know the difference between infatuation and love, and so she thought she was in love with him.

Infatuation is a state in which one person knows little about the other, but overrates the other and endows him with qualities he does not possess. It is superficial and based on an extravagant imagination. When there is physical attraction plus infatuation, it is easy for the young person to mistake this for love. Physical attraction is an essential component of heterosexual love, but there is more to the latter than this one aspect of it. Love is a feeling of friendship of such depth and power that it has moved monarchs to abdicate their thrones for it. It has its foundations in the totality of such factors as tremendous attraction, emotional maturity, willingness for mutual sharing, mutual respect, deep devotion, similar values and goals, and certain elusive factors which even scientists have not as yet been able to determine.

In an effort to impress this young man, Dolores' sister tried to make him believe that her family was quite wealthy, which it is not. A week after she returned from her vacation, he asked her to marry him. After just one conversation with the young man, Dolores' parents, with the wisdom and perceptiveness which were a product of their adult maturity, concluded that he was a liar and an irresponsible incompetent. They pleaded with their daughter not to marry him, saying that she knew little about him and what she did know was not very good; but it didn't matter.

After the wedding, the young bride became aware of her husband's sordid past, including a mass of gambling debts, which he expected his "rich" wife to pay for him. Just as her husband's past came as a surprise to Dolores' sister, so too her lack of "riches" was a blow to him; he angrily told her that she had lied to him. But he had truly deceived her. A solid, wholesome marriage is based on mutual love, on faith and trust, on consideration for each other—none of which was present here.

In a good marriage, there is mutual sharing. Here, in place of sharing, there was using of one mate by the other. Dolores' brother-in-law had never intended to support his wife; he had intended to use her to support his irresponsible behavior. In addition to the essential presence of love, the chances of marital success depend upon a number of basic factors, included among which are maturity, common interests, sense of responsibility, similar educational and other backgrounds, corresponding intellectual levels, and the financial ability to wed; this couple possessed none of these, nor did the bride and groom know much about each other.

Dolores, the "perennial pessimist," as Eddie called her, said that her sister's "marital mess" was "all the fault of fate." But was it really fate's fault that her sister had naïvely fallen for the young man's lies? Was it fate's fault that she had lied to him about her family's finances to make herself more attractive to him? Was it fate's fault that she had totally ignored her parents' pleas and called them "stupid" for having recognized the young man for what he really was?

No, it was not fate's fault. It will do Dolores' sister absolutely no good to evade the issue and blame fate or anyone but herself. On the contrary, blaming fate will be harmful to her, for it will prevent her from facing up to her shortcomings, from learning from her unpleasant experience, and from changing her ways. If she does not face up to reality after the dissolution of this unfortunate marriage, she may someday repeat the same kind of sad situation.

## MULTIPLE-DATING

Not all young people are as lacking in self-respect as Nancy, as troubled by feelings of rejection as Frankie or as naïve as Dolores' sister. Jimmy and Alice found that they were attracted to each other, but that they were ill at ease in each other's presence. Jimmy was the best math student in their class, but had difficulties with his French; Alice excelled in French, but struggled with math. When Jimmy offered to help her with her math and asked her to help him with his French, she was hesitant at first.

When Alice realized that Jimmy needed her as much as she needed him, she agreed. She admired him for his excellence in math, and her high regard for him did much to bolster his ego. This bolstering was good for Jimmy, who lacked self-confidence.

As this feeling of self-worth grew, he became more expansive and more expressive, and he could tell her how well her hair looked, how pretty her dress was, or make some other favorable comment. His esteem for her, in turn, helped Alice become more sure of herself and to be more at ease with him. Since she had found it difficult to trust others, this was a great step forward for Alice.

Although Alice and Jimmy are very fond of each other, they are both wise enough to know that they have much growing up ahead of them and a great deal to learn. They do not wish to form too serious an attachment. Like many young people their age, they enjoy multiple-dating with other couples.

In multiple-dating, each girl and boy in the group has an opportunity to observe, to listen, to share in the conversation and to learn from the others, at the same time feeling secure with his (or her) own date for the evening. In such group situations, each member tends to develop greater poise and dexterity in interpersonal, boy-girl relationships.

Among the group of boys and girls with whom Alice and Jimmy have multiple-dated is Charlie of the Tender Ten. Under Charlie's positive influence, the other young people have become convinced of the health and social benefits which can be derived from active participation in athletic activities. Jimmy and Alice have played tennis, gone bowling and have improved their skills in these sports. They have joined the school hiking club and found this group exercise invigorating.

With their increased proficiency in these wholesome, healthful group activities, Jimmy's and Alice's individual self-confidence has been soaring, and their self-mastery has been improving. Thus, like Charlie, but unlike many other young people of their age group, they have begun to feel sufficiently adequate and self-assured to make it unnecessary for them to seek and assume false, unwholesome symbols of status and security.

## THE SEARCH FOR SECURITY AND STATUS

When people are insecure, when they have little feeling of self-acceptance, when their needs are not satisfied, their sense of values may become distorted and they may tend to search for security through worthless symbols of status. This is true for young, middle-aged and old alike.

Three status symbols which have become especially significant to young people are cars, drinking and smoking. A car is an important means of transportation. When it is purchased less for that purpose and more for the purpose of impressing, and thereby hopefully becoming more popular with, relatives, acquaintances and neighbors, then the purchaser has a problem. His problem is how to cope with his feelings of inadequacy and inferiority.

Studies have shown that car ownership by teen-agers tends to have a negative effect on schoolwork, and marks start on a downward trend. Educators and other authorities generally favor parental ownership and control of the family car and advocate that teen-agers who are well-trained and licensed to drive should do so with guidance and regulation by their parents.

On the whole, the teen-ager's reflexes tend to be better than the older person's. Many teen-agers are potentially as competent drivers as many adults, if they have sufficient maturity, a sense of responsibility, and have successfully completed an approved course in driver education.

Problems arise when teen-agers, all too often, use cars as

a prop for weak egos and to make a show of themselves. Surveys have indicated that the accident rate among teen-age drivers is much higher than it is among adult drivers. Dangers especially exist when teen-agers mix drinking with driving. Their judgment and recently acquired driving ability are impaired, and of course accidents follow.

Young people start to drink—and to smoke too—for a number of reasons, chiefly because of their desire to feel important, to rebel against parental authority, to pretend they are older, to try to combat their feelings of inadequacy, and to find security and status by doing what their "crowd" is doing. Long after these reasons have ceased to exist, the drinker and the smoker may have become so addicted to these habits that they find them difficult to break.

Since social drinking in varying degrees has become acceptable in certain communities and in different levels of society, drinking among teen-agers often starts at home. Many educators and other authorities disapprove of drinking by teen-agers except under parental supervision; others disapprove of it entirely. Among a group of teen-age boys who were asked whether they drink and, if so, why, those that did drink said they did so "to go along with the crowd," but they agreed with the nondrinkers that they did not want the girls they dated to drink.

Where either parent is an alcoholic, not only is this a source of embarrassment to the teen-ager in the family, but he often worries about whether he too will suffer from this illness. Eddie's reactions to his father's alcoholism include his need for extreme immaculateness in his attire. The slightest speck of dirt or dust on any of his garments disturbs him and must be removed immediately. Good grooming is important at all age levels; pride in appearance often accompanies pride in performance. However, when this is carried to extremes, the excessive impeccability may be symptomatic of feelings of inner uncleanliness. People who feel that they are soiled or unclean within may go to great lengths externally to have their garments and other items in their surroundings absolutely spotless. Eddie should discuss his problem with his school counselor. Many chapters of Alcoholics Anonymous have teen divisions for children of alcoholics, and Eddie could be aided by his local chapter too.

Recent research studies have proven conclusively that the smoking habit is a major health hazard and that cigarettes are directly linked to lung cancer and heart disease. Many adults who have been smoking for a number of years wish they had never started; some confirmed smokers have succeeded in breaking the habit, but others who would like to do this have found it hard to accomplish. It is easier not to start smoking!

If you want all the scientific proof behind the reasons why you should not smoke, ask your school librarian or the librarian in your local public library to let you read a copy of the *Report of the Surgeon General's Advisory Committee on Smoking and Health,* published in 1964 by the United States Public Health Service.

Be kind to yourself—don't smoke! Nothing is more important to you than your health—don't ruin it! If you have already begun to smoke, make every effort to stop now.

To many young people the cigarette represents a way of saying to the world, "See, I am now a grownup." What the young smoker really is saying to the world, however, is, "I have not yet grown up, but with this cigarette in my mouth, I am hoping that I look grown up."

Well, neither that cigarette nor alcohol will help you be grown up or look grown up, but they will adversely affect your health. Neither will give you that feeling of self-worth for which you are searching. You have many good qualities and do not need to resort to these artificial, unhealthy status symbols. You can develop your feelings of self-esteem and self-respect by bringing out your good qualities, by taking advantage of your positive potentials, by using your untapped inner resources and by showing concern and doing something of value for others.

If you find that you cannot comfortably contend with this

search for security and status, for self-worth and self-respect, and are unable to resolve it to your satisfaction, remember that many your age (and older, too) have this problem, and many are unable to contend with it successfully, so you are not alone.

Discuss the problem with your parents. If you need further assistance, discuss it with your school counselor or psychologist, your family physician or your clergyman; these are professionally competent people who understand your problems and who are ready to guide you, to strengthen you and to help you build your self-esteem. This guidance, strength and increased self-esteem will aid you too as you come closer to making choices regarding the career and/or college world which awaits you.

# 10

# THE CHOICE IS YOURS

IN THIS GREAT DEMOCRACY OF OURS, YOU HAVE
the privilege of choosing your future life's work. The choice is
truly yours. Be thankful that you live in a country where, among
our many other freedoms, we have freedom of career choice
and that you may, of your own free will, make your own vocational decisions depending upon your individual abilities, personality traits, interests, ambitions, motivations and desires for
further training.

## CHALLENGES AHEAD

The world of work is a challenging, fascinating, adventurous
world. Whether you enter this world after your high school
graduation or a few years later after your graduation from college, you have ahead of you a working span of approximately
forty to forty-five years. This figure is somewhat less for females
than for males, but in view of the continuing trend for women
to return to and remain in the labor force, it has become just
as important for girls, as it is for boys, to choose their careers
conscientiously and to plan their careers carefully.

World War II brought with it a social upheaval in this country in the relationship between women and the working world.

150

In March 1940 (pre-World War II), there were 13,840,000 women employed in our national work force; twenty-five years later, in March 1965, there were about 26,000,000 women workers. Women constitute one out of every three workers today, and approximately one-third of all of the married women in the United States are employed. It is anticipated that by 1975, nearly half of all the women in this country between the ages of thirty-five and sixty-five will either be employed or seeking employment. Thus, girls and boys alike should give thoughtful consideration to their future occupations.

You can spend your many years of employment at work which not only will be financially fruitful, but will enable you to live a satisfying, useful, meaningful life, a life in which you could make worthwhile contributions to your family, your community and your country.

Today, as never before, a multitude of ever increasing educational and vocational challenges are yours. To get the greatest benefits from these, after you have gotten to know yourself better, you now must become better acquainted with the working world and all that it has to offer you.

## THE WIDE, WIDE WORLD OF WORK

There are some 30,000 different occupations in the mid-twentieth-century world of work in the United States. These occupations, on the basis of the amount of training required for entry into them and the nature of the work performed, may be classified as follows: unskilled, semiskilled, skilled, service, agricultural, clerical, sales, and technical, administrative and professional. These categories are not rigid, and some occupations may overlap from one category to another, but they do enable us to get a clearer view of the many occupational opportunities in this country.

The "labor force" of our nation consists of those who are actively employed and those who, although they are unemployed, are actively seeking employment. Approximately half a century ago, unskilled laborers constituted about twelve and a half per cent of the total labor force of our nation. This proportion has been declining steadily and is expected to continue to decline; in the mid-1960s unskilled laborers numbered about 3,500,000 and made up only about five per cent of our labor force.

The *unskilled occupations* require no special training or, at most, very minimal training. Unskilled workers generally perform manual tasks involving heavy physical labor. Tremendous technological progress and automation have made vast inroads into the fields where unskilled laborers had been employed, and mechanized equipment (such as conveyor belts, cranes and hoists) has replaced many of these men. The increasing complexity of our automated age calls for workers who are trained and possess specific higher levels of skill.

*Semiskilled occupations,* in the main, require a limited amount of training, and often this training is obtained on the job. Known too as "operatives," since they often operate a machine of some kind, semiskilled workers together make up the largest occupational group in our country's labor force. Generally, they work with their hands, doing routine, repetitive operations. Young people seeking work in a semiskilled occupation should enjoy doing the same things over and over again and be capable of carefully following instructions.

There were more than 12,000,000 semiskilled workers in the United States in the mid-1960s, and among them they included the truck drivers, bus drivers, taxi drivers, sewing machine operators, assemblers, inspectors, power truck operators, production painters, stationary (boiler) firemen and machine tool operators.

Young people who have mechanical aptitude and like to work with their hands will find a vast number of opportunities for employment among the great many semiskilled and skilled occupations. Although employment prospects appear favorable in the semiskilled occupations as we continue on into the latter

1960s, the greatest opportunities of all will be in the skilled and technical occupations and in the professional and other white-collar fields. In this technological and scientific age, specialized training has come to be the "passport to employment."

The *skilled occupations* are also known as the "crafts," and therefore skilled workers are also called craftsmen. Because of their additional training, skilled workers serve under less supervision than semiskilled workers, and they may be called upon to exercise more judgment than the latter. Craftsmen learn their trades by way of apprenticeships or through specialized vocational training during or after their high school years. The Armed Forces too offer vocational programs by means of which young men and young women may acquire skills which will be of value in their future civilian employment. Interestingly, whereas women constitute approximately one-third of all of the semiskilled workers, they make up only a small proportion of the total number of skilled workers in this country.

Since World War II, the job trend in the skilled occupations has been an upward one. There were approximately 5,000,000 craftsmen in 1940. By the mid-1960s, their number had risen to close to 9,000,000. They include the carpenters, who represent the largest single group of all the craftsmen, and the automobile mechanics, painters and paper hangers, welders and oxygen cutters, plumbers and pipe fitters, all-round mechanics, bricklayers, electricians (maintenance and construction), operating engineers, stationary engineers, industrial machinery repairmen, appliance servicemen, tool and die makers, sheet-metal workers and a variety of other smaller groups of miscellaneous skilled workers.

For more information about apprenticeships and/or specific apprenticeable trades, get in touch with your State Apprenticeship Council, if there is one in your state, or your Regional Office of the Bureau of Apprenticeship and Training, or write directly to the U. S. Department of Labor, Bureau of Apprenticeship and Training, Washington, D.C.

The *service occupations* include those in which the workers directly serve the public. In the main, these services either increase the public's comforts and conveniences or protect their lives and properties. There are today about 9,000,000 people engaged in the service occupations, and they may be divided into four groups: (1) domestic service workers, (2) protective service workers, (3) personal service workers and (4) business and industrial workers.

The domestic service workers are known too as private household workers and include the butlers, caretakers, chambermaids, cooks, housekeepers, kitchen helpers, laundresses, maids, nursemaids, valets, window cleaners and a miscellany of other general household helpers who work in private homes and residences. Guards and watchmen, policemen and detectives, F.B.I. agents and firemen compose the vast majority of the civilian protective service workers. Under the heading of personal service workers come barbers, beauty operators, practical nurses, auxiliary nursing workers and airline stewardesses. Among the business and industrial service workers are the bellhops, bus boys and bus girls, cooks and chefs, dishwashers, elevator operators, hat check girls, janitors, porters, theatre ushers and waiters and waitresses.

The nature of the work performed in the many different service occupations varies greatly from one occupation to another and so too does the amount of education required for entry, which ranges from some high school plus limited specialized training to a college degree. Service workers should have a pleasant manner and possess the ability to get along well with others. With the exception of elevator operators, whose jobs are being eliminated by automatically operated elevators, and theatre ushers, for whom there is less demand today because television has caused a decline in the number of motion picture theatres, employment opportunities in the service occupations are expected to rise throughout the remainder of the 1960s and into the early 1970s.

*Agricultural occupations* have undergone vast changes due to the technological revolution which has taken place on the farm and in the farming industry in the United States. A century ago, more than half of the people in this country were employed in the field of agriculture. Today less than eight per cent of our total civilian labor force is working on farms. Similarly, about a hundred years ago, the average farm worker could produce enough food for only about five persons, whereas today's average farmer is able to supply the food needs of himself and twenty-six other people.

In the past several years, modern mechanization has been rapidly displacing farm labor, and employment opportunities for farm workers have been steadily declining. There are today somewhat more than 5,000,000 people employed on farms, and it is anticipated that by 1975 this number will be reduced by about a million. It is important to note, however, that this decline in the number of farm workers has been accompanied by a marked increase in the number of workers employed off the farm in vocations allied to agriculture. The latter are known as nonfarm agricultural occupations.

Nonfarm agricultural workers are found in farm supply stores, farm machinery industries, feed mills, fertilizer plants, food processing plants and a variety of other businesses which process, distribute or transport farm products and farm supplies.

Vocational agriculture programs are offered in many high schools throughout the country to prepare young people for careers in farming or in one of the nonfarm agricultural occupations. Many of the latter are professional or technical in nature and require specialized college training. It is desirable that workers in most agricultural occupations—"on-the-farm" and "off-the-farm"—have a love for the outdoors and for plant and animal life, be capable of operating mechanical equipment and have a knowledge of agricultural science.

With the *clerical occupations,* we enter the wide world of the white-collar workers. (Those in the sales, and technical, administrative and professional occupations are also considered white-collar workers.) Some 10,000,000 people are engaged in varied forms of recordkeeping, paperwork and other clerical activities. Among these millions are the secretarial workers (typists, stenographers, secretaries), bookkeeping workers (bookkeepers, bookkeeping clerks, bookkeeping machine operators), office machine operators, electronic computer operators, mail clerks and carriers, telephone operators, bank tellers, airline ticket agents, cashiers and a varied assortment of other office workers. Approximately two-thirds of the total number of clerical workers are women.

The high school diploma is often the basic educational requirement for most clerical positions. The completion of commercial and business courses, either as part of the high school program or in addition to it, is desirable too. Clerical workers generally perform their duties in offices with many other employees and, therefore, should be capable of getting along well with their fellow workers, have a pleasant disposition, speak well and make a neat, clean appearance.

Although automation is making inroads into some of the clerical fields, it has no appreciable effect on the great many clerical positions which call for contact with the public. On the whole, future prospects for employment in clerical positions appear to be very favorable, especially so for those who possess secretarial, stenographic and/or typing skills.

The *sales occupations* cover all sorts of workers who earn their incomes by selling miscellaneous products and services. There are today about 4,500,000 salespeople. Approximately ninety per cent of these sales workers serve as salespeople in retail stores, salespeople in wholesale trade, manufacturers' sales representatives, insurance agents and brokers, and real estate salesmen and brokers.

The amount and nature of the education required for entry into a sales career vary greatly according to the products and services being sold. Although a high school diploma is generally the minimum requirement for most sales positions, little knowledge or ability is required of the girl who stands behind the counter of a retail variety store and simply "waits" on customers. However, those who sell technical products and special services often need a college degree; also, they should speak properly and be conversant in all specialized aspects of that which they are selling. Persuasive ability, tact, a pleasant manner and a desire to work with people are essential attributes for potential salespeople. Many signs point to the prospect of a continuing upward trend in sales volume, and thus the employment future looks bright in the selling fields.

The *technical, administrative and professional occupations* collectively contain the most highly educated members of our national labor force, although there are some professional occupations in the creative and performance fields which can be entered with less than a college degree. The *technical occupations* are closely allied to the professions and include those of the varied technicians who work in cooperation with scientists, engineers and other professional personnel. In the *administrative occupations* are found a multiplicity of managers, administrators and executives of many sorts, including self-employed business proprietors. In the *professional occupations,* there are those who need one or more college or university degrees, such as the accountants, clergymen, dentists, engineers, lawyers, librarians, physicians, psychologists, school counselors and teachers, and those who possess special creative talent and/or performing ability, such as the actor, artist and ballet dancer.

There is great diversity in the nature of the work performed by the persons in the many different technical, administrative and professional occupations. Thus, the personal characteristics desirable for entry vary with each one of these occupations. In the main, they require the determination to undertake long periods of specialized preparation and the ability to be accepted into and to successfully complete such programs of preparation.

There are about 7,500,000 people who earn their livelihood by engaging in some form of administrative activities and about 8,000,000 who are members of the technical-professional occupations. Although the specific proportion of women in these vocations varies with each individual occupation, the number of women in technical, administrative and professional positions has been steadily increasing.

As we enter the latter half of the 1960s and go on into the 1970s, it is expected that of all the occupational groups, the greatest growth in employment opportunities will take place within this group, known collectively as the technical, administrative and professional occupations.

Our nation's population explosion, the spectacular proliferation of our storehouse of knowledge and the consequent development of new professional and technical fields are causing an unprecedented demand for highly trained professional personnel. The intensified complexity of our modern technology has created a growing need for increased numbers of college-trained specialists, and employment opportunities for tomorrow's college graduates look bright indeed.

Young men—and young women too—should give serious thought to the career opportunities and training facilities available to them in the United States Armed Forces. For the latest information on military obligations and opportunities in each of the services, write to the U. S. Department of Defense, Washington, D. C.

## MANY OUT OF MANY

With all these occupational groups and so many thousands of different occupations from among which to make a selection, choosing a career seems like a formidable task to many young people. "How do you select the one that's best for you when there are thousands to pick?" asked Eddie of his school counselor.

Well, happily, there is no *one* which is best for you. There are *many* at which you could succeed and which would provide you with satisfying, useful careers.

With the necessary education and specialized training, you may be capable of doing well in several occupations within the same field and also in several occupations in different fields. This is fortunate too because in our complex, quickly changing world, you will probably not be working at *one* but at *several* different occupations during your working lifetime. In your long-range career planning, you must, however, give much consideration to your choice of the primary occupation which will be your key to entry into the working world. Next to choice of mate, this is one of the most important decisions you will be called upon to make. Use care, caution and common sense in choosing that career.

Many factors affect your vocational decision. Among these are your abilities, aptitudes, personality traits, interests, individual motivation and a multitude of variable circumstances within your family and community. Your personality traits not only influence your career choice, but also play an important part in your progress in a particular position. More people lose jobs because of negative personality traits than for any other causes.

Many shifts and changes are taking place in the working world in our rapidly changing space age. These and many other factors in your immediate environment and in the national and international scene may affect your vocational decision and influence you toward one special initial occupation rather than toward any others. Since there are also many unpredictable elements which suddenly may need to be considered in this important decision-making, it is wise to allow for flexibility in your long-range career planning.

Deciding upon the vocational fields for which you may be best suited and in which you show the greatest promise for success is a difficult task calling for serious thought and planning. It often calls too for competent assistance from qualified counselors. If you have questions—and most young people do—about your vocational future, make an appointment to see your school counselor. He will not make a career choice for you. It is for YOU to make this decision.

Your school counselor will, however, help you to understand yourself better, to become more aware of your strengths and weaknesses and to appreciate why your personality traits and mental abilities and aptitudes and interests and all else about you tend to incline you more toward certain types of work than others. From him too, you will be able to learn more about the working world; he can provide you with a good deal of general occupational information plus pertinent information about many specific occupations. With your school counselor's assistance, you will be equipped to make a wiser vocational decision.

Eddie does not want to go to college. He is interested in mechanics and would like to become an airplane mechanic. The very thought of this was intolerable to his mother, who was eager to have him attend a four-year college. Eddie discussed his problem with his counselor, who called the mother in for consultation. After several counseling and testing sessions, Eddie decided that he would apply for admission to a two-year technical institute after his high school graduation; he concluded that someday he might like to work on rockets and spaceships and that, therefore, the additional two years of technical training would be of value to him in the future, as well as in the present. Since his mother had become more aware of her son's motivations and inclinations through the consultation sessions, she became more tolerant toward his vocational choice and accepted his decision to attend a technical institute.

So much of your future—how you will earn your living, where you will work, how much you will earn, where and how you will live, in which social circles you will travel and, possibly even, whom you will marry—depends to such a great extent upon your choice of career. Your long-range plans for your vocational tomorrows similarly depend so much upon your basic personality characteristics. Are you the kind of person who must get your way and get it today?

## URGENTLY NEEDED—A HIGH SCHOOL DIPLOMA

Some young people insist that they must have what they want immediately. They have no interest in long-range plans. They have no desire to plan for tomorrow. Today concerns them, they say, and it is today that they want to enter the working world. Thousands of high school dropouts felt this way, but with the passage of time, they sadly discovered that today is the tomorrow for which they did not plan yesterday.

All too often, for the dropouts, their todays are now hollow days of unemployment or, at best, underemployment. Your job now is to stay in school; if you leave school without a high school diploma you may have no job later.

Today, in our automated, scientific space age, in order to enter the world of work young people must be far more skilled than were those of past generations. The unemployment rolls have become bloated with unskilled, untrained young people looking for work. Some years ago, it was possible for a young person to tell a prospective employer that he was willing to do "anything" and then be hired for some unskilled job. Automation, technological advances and increased efficiency in business management have brought a decline in the need for unskilled workers.

Now, when a candidate for employment says he is willing to do "anything," the personnel interviewer or prospective employer interprets this to mean that he is capable of doing "nothing." He is, therefore, not hired, because today the job applicant must be capable of doing "something." He must be trained and equipped to do something specific.

Today's young person must have a marketable skill to offer

a prospective employer. To acquire this marketable skill, you must have that basic high school diploma. During the decade of the 1960s, 26,000,000 young people below the age of twenty-five will be entering the national labor force. Competition for jobs for untrained young people is keen and will become ever keener as we proceed toward the 1970s. The possession of a high school diploma plus a marketable skill is a minimum necessity as your safeguard against unemployment.

Many who drop out of high school give as one of their reasons that to them school is "kid stuff." Well, they are only "kidding" themselves. It is not the ones who remain in school who are the "kids"; the real "kids" are those who quit. The tot demands his pleasure today, right now; "tomorrow" has no meaning to him. The dropout is like this "kid" who must have his lollipop immediately, except that the dropout's "lollipop" is a record player or fancy clothes or a car.

One of the first signs of maturity is the ability to forego a minor pleasure today in favor of a major pleasure tomorrow, to defer gratification. The immature dropout faces a future of low-paid, unsatisfying jobs riddled with many periods of unemployment. Your high school diploma will provide you with far greater pleasure in your many future tomorrows than that temporary, limited pleasure which the dropout derives from deserting his school desk today.

Act mature! Stay in school! Get that high school diploma and develop a marketable skill which will make you a desirable job applicant and an asset to a prospective employer. If your desire to leave school stems from financial or other personal or school problems, don't drop out—do drop in to your school counselor's office. Consult with your counselor. He is in a position to help you. Whatever you say to your counselor is held in strict confidence, so you may feel free to discuss your problems with him. Speak with him. Cooperate with him. He will work with you and do whatever is best to ease your problems and make your school life pleasanter and more productive.

## AFTER HIGH SCHOOL—WHAT?

All high school students, long before their graduation day, must decide whether they will seek full-time employment or college admission after completing their high school programs. Even before you entered high school, you were compelled to come to a tentative decision regarding your future career and to determine whether this career choice called for a college education.

Possibly you concluded that you did not want to go to college and chose the commercial or vocational curriculum. If you did, it is important for you to know that the completion of a commercial or vocational high school program does not necessarily bar you from a future college education, if you should at some later date decide that you would like to go to college. There are colleges which accept graduates of such high school programs, depending upon what it is you would like to study at college. Should you decide later that you would like to matriculate for a degree at a college which has academic course requirements for admission, you could make up these deficiencies by returning to a day high school or enrolling in an evening or summer session to complete the courses you lack.

High school students who have decided not to continue on to college should read this writer's *Your Career—If You're Not Going to College* (published by Julian Messner). In this book, you will find much information about a great many occupational opportunities open to the noncollege-bound. Additionally, college-bound, as well as noncollege-bound, students will learn from reading this book the step-by-step scientific process for making tentative and long-range vocational decisions and also how to obtain, enter upon and progress in the specific positions for which you have prepared; it should aid you too in seeking and finding part-time and summertime jobs.

When you entered high school, perhaps you decided upon a

particular profession which calls for a college degree (or two or more degrees, as is now the case for many professions) and you enrolled in the academic high school curriculum. Then too, perhaps you embarked on an academic program because you decided that you would like to continue on into college despite the fact that you had not as yet reached any decision about your vocational future.

It is perfectly all right if you have not yet made any specific occupational judgments, for there is much you need to learn about yourself, about the working world in general and about specific career opportunities before you come to wise vocational decisions. Upon these decisions will rest the amount and nature of the further education which you will need to reach your long-range goals.

## THE CALL TO COLLEGE

More and more young people are answering "the call to college." Not everyone needs to go to college; not everyone should go to college. But you should and can continue on into college if you have the capacity and desire to enter upon and complete a college curriculum. The knowledge you acquire at college will kindle your imagination and lead you into intellectual adventures that will stimulate and challenge your mental faculties. If you have the ability to do college work, you need the knowledge and training which comes from a college education in order to use that mental ability to the fullest.

No matter how much mental ability you possess, unless this ability has been challenged, trained and sharpened in specific areas of higher endeavor, you will not be able to fulfill your potential nor to participate in satisfying our great national need for professional and technical personnel.

This is a fascinating world in which we live, and your college education will enable you all the better to understand, appreciate and partake of its many wonders. There are positive personal pleasures to be derived from the pursuit of knowledge and the process of learning.

The number of young people seeking admission to college is mounting. College costs are climbing. Competition for financial aid is becoming increasingly keener. You may be wondering and asking whether you can defy these rising forces. The answer is, "Yes, you can." You can get a college education if you are capable and deserving.

Today, as never before, the government, colleges and universities and a multitude of sponsors of financial aid are ready to help students who are able and needy, who are qualified and worthy. If you are concerned about meeting the costs of your college education, read this writer's *Your College Education— How to Pay for It* (published by Julian Messner). This book tells you how you can decrease your college costs, increase your financial resources and obtain financial aid if financial need exists; also, it offers you a great deal of information on varied sources of financial aid.

There is mounting demand for technical and professional personnel. Our nation needs increasing numbers of college graduates trained in the fields of health, education, engineering, science, government service and numerous other specialties. If you have the ability and ambition for a college education, you can help yourself by going to college—and, our country, our institutions of higher education and a vast variety of sponsoring organizations and individuals stand ready to help you if you need and are worthy of financial assistance.

Dolores wants to become a nurse. However, there are several school-age children in her family, and she believed her father could not afford to pay for her higher education. Her counselor, therefore, informed her that because there is a great shortage of nurses, her state government is offering assistance to any student who has the ability to become a nurse and who needs financial aid in order to undertake the training program. He also gave her information about several organizations which aid prospective nurses. Dolores is becoming more hopeful about someday being a nurse.

It is especially important to remember that college is a place of learning, a place wherein you should grow and mature. College should not be converted into a status symbol in an attempt to impress relatives, friends and neighbors. Your college choice should not be based on false prestige factors. The three or four colleges to which you may ultimately seek admission should be selected on the basis of which ones offer you the best opportunities to develop your mental abilities, your special talents, your interests, your personality traits and all of your potentialities to the fullest.

It is well to bear in mind that if you pay higher tuition fees it does not necessarily mean you will receive a better education. In the main, there is little, if any, relationship between the total costs of a college education and the quality of that education. There are numerous excellent low-cost institutions of higher education just as there are numerous excellent high-cost institutions. Essentially—and do not forget this—regardless of which college you attend, you will get out of college exactly what you put into it. What you put into it will depend greatly upon your emotional maturity.

# 11
# MARCHING TOWARD MATURITY

EMOTIONAL MATURITY IS THE ULTIMATE GOAL OF each person's growth and development. It is a dynamic process involving perpetual progress. We must persist at this growth progress throughout our lives. What is this goal, this process, this progress? What is emotional maturity?

## THE MEANING OF MATURITY

Emotional maturity is the ability to adjust, wholesomely and harmoniously, to your surroundings and to the problems presented by and in these surroundings. It is not a fixed destination at which you arrive and remain. It is a pathway along which you proceed, properly and appropriately adjusting to the exigencies along the way. As changes occur within us and in our external environment, we must constantly adjust and readjust to these changes. The mature person is the one who can adapt rationally and realistically to the changed circumstances in his life as each need arises. Maturity involves making many compromises with life.

Life calls upon us often to alter, to add to or to subtract from our attitudes, our feelings, our habits, our ideas, our thoughts and our varied modes of behavior. We must continue to grow, to improve, to advance, to adapt every year, every month, every week, every day of our lives. Maturity embraces this ample, healthy adjustment to our environment and to the constant changes which occur in our internal and external surroundings.

A child of five may be quite mature for his age. The next year, at the age of six, he may no longer be "mature for his age" unless he progressed and developed commensurately during that year. Thus, too, you may have been wholesomely adjusted— mature—at ten. However, unless you continued to advance, to thrive and to make progress since then, you may not be very mature today.

Each of the Tender Ten can become more mature; they can become better adjusted, more cooperative group members. They can relate to each other in a more wholesome fashion. Some of them have problems which are relatively minor, and they may be able to help themselves; several have more serious problems and need the assistance of their school counselor or psychologist; others are troubled by problems of even greater severity, and out-of-school professional assistance may be needed.

All of them can be helped to make better adjustment to their surroundings. All of them can change, improve and become more socially acceptable. The Tender Ten can have a successful project if they would learn to cooperate, to compromise and to respect the rights of others as much as they wish theirs respected; they can learn to do these things if they would make the effort to do so.

Glimpses into the pasts of the Tender Ten were presented to show you how and why personalities develop in certain directions and some of the influences which act on the development of individual personalities. Space limitations have only allowed for the presentation of certain highlights in the backgrounds of each of these young people. It must be remembered, however, that all personalities are exceedingly complex and that vast and varied forces act upon all of us to tend to make us what we are.

These forces influence each individual's progress toward maturity.

It must be stressed here that each person is an individual, and we should not jump to conclusions on the basis of generalities. Dolores comes from a large family and is pessimistic, but not everyone who comes from a large family is thus disposed; many from large families are optimistic, and many from small families are pessimistic. Susie is an only child and is exceedingly spoiled, but, as I said earlier, not every only child is spoiled, and not everyone who is spoiled is an only child. These are individual reactions, and Dolores and Susie have reacted on the basis of all of the forces and factors which have influenced them throughout their lives. This is how their "nature" reacted with their "nurture."

It is important here too to re-emphasize what has been said before, that rarely are the experiences of one's early years so shattering that the damages cannot be mended or nullified as the person grows older. So, whatever your problems, don't blame your past. Don't blame society. Don't blame fate. Don't blame your parents. If you would like to take several slaps at the face of the one most responsible for your problems—don't—your cheeks would sting too much!

Henry Wadsworth Longfellow in his *Hyperion* said, "Look not mournfully into the Past. It comes not back again. Wisely improve the Present. It is thine."

Face up to your present problems. You have many positive attributes. You have your own unique potentials and special inner resources and talents. Use them! Develop them to as full a capacity as you can. Many men and women of renown have risen above extreme difficulties, disappointments and disadvantaged backgrounds and have overcome numerous hardships and handicaps to achieve success. They adjusted, they grew, they reacted realistically—they matured. You can too. Whatever your problems, you can rise above them and conquer them. Yes, you too can be successful. But, first, you must understand what it means to be successful.

## YOU CAN BE SUCCESSFUL

"Success" is one of the most misused words in the English language. So many people think it means earning a sumptuous salary and possessing fancy furs, jewels, cars and, perhaps too, a mansion on a mountaintop. Well this is *not*—emphatically *not* —success. Don't misunderstand—I am not saying that those who have these possessions are necessarily failures. They too may be successful. I am saying that these are not the elements which constitute success. Psychologists and psychiatrists are all too aware of so many people who have lots of money and many material things, but who are unhappy, troubled failures.

What then is success? Success is self-fulfillment. What is self-fulfillment? It is that inner glow, that personal gratification, which comes to you when you know that you have done something well and that what you have done has served a useful purpose.

If your standards of individual values are satisfied and these values are ethically, morally and legally acceptable, and if your work and your life give you a feeling of accomplishment, of personal achievement, you are a success. Success is a personal matter. The successful person is satisfied with and gratified by his activities and performances.

The person who is a success has a sense of belonging, of being needed, of filling a significant niche in our society. This is not smug self-satisfaction, but rather an emotionally mature, humble sense of accomplishment which develops from doing something of value that needs to be done, something you enjoy doing and doing it well. The tailor who owns the small shop on Main Street and who achieves that delightful feeling of inner contentment from the competency with which he completes his customers' suits is a successful man. The show business celebrity with fabulous earnings who must consume countless sleeping pills to escape from his privately troubled world into a bit of tranquil slumber is a dismal failure.

Success is built upon the foundations of many personal qualities—perseverance, hard work, initiative, drive, self-discipline, self-respect, a sense of responsibility and a striving for what you think is right. It also calls for confidence in yourself and faith in a higher being. In his Inaugural Address on January 20, 1965, President Lyndon B. Johnson said, "If we succeed, it will not be because of what we have, but it will be because of what we are; not because of what we own, but rather because of what we believe."

There are those who prefer to avoid the hard work which is so necessary to achieve success and who seek ready excuses for their own failures; these people invariably attribute the successes of others to "luck." But, ah no—the great accomplishments, inventions and discoveries of this world have not been due to luck. Serendipity, yes; but luck, no!

What is serendipity? Serendipity is the occurrence of unexpected happy accidents for which a person is prepared because of years of training and hard work. An actor leaves his role and his understudy takes his place. For the understudy, this is an "unexpected happy accident," but the understudy succeeds only if he has practiced and rehearsed and rigorously prepared for the role. Thus, the understudy who becomes a star is not "lucky"; he is serendipital. The scientist who studies for a great many years and then after months and months of seemingly endless experimentation arrives at an "unexpected happy accident," which provides him with the answer he has been seeking, is not "lucky"; he too is serendipital. If not for his studies and his diligent, enduring research, the "happy accident" which occurred in his test tube would have gone unnoticed and been meaningless to him.

Yes, there is a big difference between luck and serendipity. The difference is the presence of persistent hard work, patient preparation, practice and perseverance. There are those who spend their years waiting to get a "lucky break"; they wait and dream for a pack of golden pay and all they get is old and gray.

Yes, you can be successful. You have far more capabilities, far more potentials, than you put to use. To be successful, to realize your potentials, you must be informed. To be informed means to be educated. This does not mean, however, that to be successful you must necessarily have a college education. Here again, we have come to a word which is so often misused, the word "education."

Essentially, education is the search for truth, the search for knowledge, to enable us to live better and fuller lives. *Veritas,* the Latin word for "truth," is firmly entrenched in the mottoes of colleges and universities throughout the nation. This search for truth goes on in many different places and in many different ways. The college campus is not the only place where knowledge may be acquired. Whether you ultimately decide to discontinue your formal schooling after you receive your high school diploma or whether you continue on to college, whether you enter upon a career which does not call for a college degree or whether you enter upon one which does, you can, in any case, become an educated person.

Who is an educated person? He is the informed, the alert, the aware person. He is the person who is constantly searching for knowledge, for truth. Education must be a lifelong process if we are to keep up with the ever changing events of the world, events which closely touch our personal lives. The college graduate who ceases his search for truth after he receives his degree ceases also to be an educated person. The high school graduate, without a college degree, can be an educated person if he continues to keep himself informed and intellectually alert.

In our democratic society, vast learning opportunities are available to all today as never before, and it is the responsibility of all citizens to take advantage of these opportunities. With the reduction in the hours of work, people have much more leisure time than they had in the past. This time could be well spent, educationally, by reading good books, magazines and newspapers. Good reading matter helps to extend your fund of information, enlarge your vocabulary and develop your reasoning power. Free public libraries, school libraries, lending libraries and book clubs of all sorts have helped to bring learning within easy reach of all of us.

Radio and television also help to keep us alert and aware. They bring news and a miscellany of information right into your own home. You can attend lectures and participate in the discussions which follow at your local church or synagogue, "Y" or community center; these will guide you in formulating intelligent opinions and goad you into wholesome action where you might otherwise have remained inactive.

Other excellent sources of knowledge, after your high school days have ended, are the evening adult education classes conducted by many of the public libraries in the larger cities. The evening session divisions of many high schools, colleges and universities also offer a variety of courses for adults who are not enrolled for diplomas or degrees. Also there are recognized correspondence courses offered by a number of institutions of higher education throughout the country; a copy of "A Guide to Correspondence Study in Colleges and Universities" may be obtained by sending twenty-five cents to the Office of the Secretary, National University Extension Association, 122 Social Science Building, University of Minnesota, Minneapolis, Minnesota 55455.

Every community has further opportunities for the educational enrichment of its citizens, such as museums, exhibits, art shows, concerts, operas and theaters. All of the aforementioned offer you the chance to develop intellectually and to become a more educated person. Yes, if you make the necessary efforts, you CAN be successful and educated. You can be fulfilled and informed. YOUR success and YOUR education are interwoven with YOUR maturity, and much depends upon YOUR progress in YOUR march toward maturity.

## YOUR *MARCH TOWARD MATURITY*

As you proceed along the pathway toward maturity, there are certain basic guideposts to aid you in your progress.

*Face up to life realistically and with self-respect.* Don't poke your head into the ground; you are a human being and not an ostrich. Tackle your problems realistically and rationally. Don't keep your troubles bottled up within you; discuss them with your parents, school counselor or psychologist, family physician, clergyman or other sensible adult confidant(e). Cultivate high ideals and standards and then let your conscience guide you. Don't feel sorry for yourself; if you do, you will discover that no one else will. Have respect for yourself and give respect to others.

*Be a positive "doer."* Be an active "can do" participant, not a passive "can't do" person. Positive attitudes can produce accomplishments; negative attitudes help bring self-defeat. This world is an exciting, adventurous place. Explore and enjoy the magnificence of nature and of the man-made wonders of your environment. Immerse yourself in the fascinating, challenging youth activities which are open to you and which are of specific interest to you in your school and community. Go forward enthusiastically with your many assets and aptitudes to acceptable, meaningful achievements.

*Assume your share of responsibility.* You have increasing numbers of freedoms and privileges, but with these come responsibilities. Don't expect your parents—or others—to keep doing things for you; it is time for you to start doing more for them. Learn to be more self-reliant. The immature person is the one who does not accept his share of responsibilities and wants others to carry it for him.

*Be empathetic, not apathetic.* Be cooperative and think of others. Empathy is the ability to have compassion for another person and to "put yourself in someone else's shoes" and, thereby, to understand what he is enduring. The empathetic person has warmth and concern for humanity; the apathetic person is cold and indifferent. Have faith in people, but don't naïvely trust everyone (learn to differentiate between those whose motives are good and those whose are not!).

*Be less self-involved and more other-involved.* You can overcome the feelings of aloneness and of being unwanted, which trouble so many young people, by participating in wholesome community service projects and doing volunteer work in hospitals and similar institutions. More than 18,000,000 boys and girls throughout the United States serve as American Red Cross Youth Volunteers; others serve as Candy Stripers in hospitals, as Junior Gray Ladies, and with the teen-age volunteer divisions of the Salvation Army, United Fund Agencies, their local churches or synagogues and similar service, religious and health agencies. You can too! Your services are needed and wanted.

*Learn to love instead of wasting your energies on hate.* Edgar Guest said it beautifully in his poem, "Teach the Boy":

> "And how to build a better world?
>    Well, not by chart or plan,
>      Unless we start to teach the boy
>        To be a better man.
>    For all our dreams of nobler things
>      Will meet the same old fate,
>    Unless we turn to fellowship
>      And do away with hate."

*Start to practice self-discipline.* Replace the self-indulgence of your childhood with the self-discipline of the mature adult. Exercise self-control. The mature adult is capable of denying himself something he likes if he knows it is not good for him and of postponing a present lesser pleasure in order to have a greater pleasure at a future date. One of the most significant signs of maturity is the ability to defer gratification.

*Cultivate a sense of humor.* Be able to laugh at yourself. Life is dull and more difficult when you are humorless. With a sense of humor, we can laugh at ourselves, accept our weaknesses, know that the world is not coming to an end because we have blundered and be more tolerant of the weaknesses and blunders of others. Remember, too, as it says in the Book of Proverbs: "A merry heart doeth good like medicine, but a depressed spirit drieth up the bones."

*Promote your self-confidence.* Make the best of your abilities. Pry out your untapped positive potentials. Accept yourself and be pleased you are you. You have your strengths and weaknesses just as everyone else has. We are all capable of doing some things very well and others not so well. Develop your capabilities to their fullest. Be yourself. Don't try to be somebody else. You can do well; you can even do better. You should have a humble, healthy sense of self-satisfaction with what you can do and continue to strive to do better.

*Have healthy, wholesome positive aspirations.* As Robert Browning said, "A man's reach should exceed his grasp or what's a heaven for." Aspire to realistic, attainable, desirable goals. Be aware of your limitations, but don't let fear of failure deter you; learn from past failures so you may go on to future successes. Don't be easily discouraged. Let yourself be inspired by the many noteworthy and praiseworthy people of accomplishment in your community, in our country and throughout the world. Have a sense of purpose and a sense of direction as to where you hope to go and as to what you hope to accomplish. There is a joy in working hard for something special, in earning it and in achieving your goal. Remember that the little postage stamp reaches its destination because it sticks to its goal.

*Don't be afraid to be a nonconformist.* There are many things in life to which we must conform, but simply because your friends or schoolmates are doing a certain thing does not mean that you should do it too, if what they are doing is immoral, unethical or illegal, or even simply absurd and/or antisocial. Think before you conform. You will be much happier later on if you have the courage of your convictions now.

*Allocate adequate time daily for work, rest and play.* Don't waste time, for time is the stuff of which life is made, but don't try to cram too much into each day either. Protect your health—be sure to get sufficient sleep; proportion your time wisely too for school, study and recreation. Relax and live each day at a time. Positive achievers accomplish a great deal because they have learned to plan and manage their time wisely and well. Plan ahead, but allow for flexibility in your plans, for changes may be necessary.

*Develop good work habits and worthwhile hobbies.* At work (school and/or job) do the best you can; this will help to build your self-confidence and self-esteem. Strive for a well-balanced vocational and avocational (hobby) life. Sometimes what cannot be achieved vocationally can be accomplished avocationally. Thus, the person who cannot earn a living as an artist can practice painting as a hobby. In the future, with people spending fewer hours on their jobs, you will have more leisure time. Your general contentment and sense of satisfaction will probably then depend to a great extent upon the pleasures you derive from your avocational and community service pursuits rather than essentially upon your vocational activities.

*Have faith in God.* There are times in life when unpleasant, stressful situations arise and we have no choice but to accept them. At such times, many people have found solace in the Biblical dictum, "Thy will be done." Faith in a higher being helps people not only in time of stress, but at all times. A firm belief in universal order offers the individual a feeling of belonging to this universe, provides an inner contentment and aids in replacing despair with hope and darkness with light. At the Presidential Prayer Breakfast on February 4, 1965, President Lyndon B. Johnson said, "I find for myself—as I know men and women throughout the government also find—a sustaining strength from moments of prayer, whether we assemble together or pray silently alone."

The emotionally mature person is a mentally healthy person. Mental health is not just the absence of mental illness; it is the active, positive presence of a wholesomely adjusted, robust and vigorous personality. A healthy person is rational, realistic and relaxed. He is vibrant and vital, energetic and exuberant, and sensible and sound in body and mind. This person is full of hope, always adjusting, constantly growing, striving for self-improvement.

Seek to improve your grooming and manners, your attractiveness and alertness, your efficiency and effectiveness. Offer your labor, your loyalty and your leadership to meaningful projects. Show initiative and enthusiastic wholehearted interest in the family, school, community and country to which you belong.

We are extremely fortunate to be citizens of this great democracy of ours which provides us with vast freedoms and opportunities permitting us to fulfill our potentials and develop our inner resources to their fullest. Do your part to maintain our liberties and our democratic way of life. Volunteer your time and talents, your efforts and exuberance, to the political party of your choice to help place in public office men and women of the highest competency, compassion and commitment.

Stand up and be counted. Express yourself. You can accomplish something of value. Remember the words of the late President John F. Kennedy: "One person can make a difference and each person should try."

Yes, you can make a difference—and you should try! Become a contributing, constructive, creative member of your community and country. This will help you to live a more positive, more productive, more purposeful life and lead to the progressive enhancement, enlightenment and enrichment of *your personality* and *you.*

# SOURCES OF FURTHER INFORMATION

## A. WHAT TO READ

*All About the Human Mind.* Robert M. Goldenson. 143 pages. 1963. Random House, New York 10022.

*Dating Tips for Teens.* Lester A. Kirkendall & Ruth Farnham Osborne. 48 pages. 1962. Science Research Associates, Inc., Chicago, Ill. 60611.

*Do Your Dreams Match Your Talents?* Vance Packard. 43 pages. 1960. Science Research Associates, Inc., Chicago, Ill. 60611.

*For Young Adults Only: The Doctor Discusses Your Personal Problems.* Frank H. Richardson. 133 pages. 1961. Tupper & Love, New York 10017.

*How to Study Better and Get Higher Marks.* Eugene H. Ehrlich. 287 pages. 1961. Thomas Y. Crowell Co., New York 10016.

*"I Wish I'd Known That Before I Came to College."* 12 pages. 1963. University of Rochester, Public Relations Office, Rochester, New York 14627.

*It's Your Education.* Brother Philip Harris, Rev. William J. McMahon & James J. Cribbin. 338 pages. 1965. Harcourt, Brace & World, Inc., New York 10017.

*It's Your Future.* James J. Cribbin, Brother Philip Harris & Rev. William J. McMahon. 365 pages. 1965. Harcourt, Brace & World, Inc., New York 10017.

*It's Your Life.* James J. Cribbin, Brother Philip Harris & Rev. William J. McMahon. 333 pages. 1964. Harcourt, Brace & World, Inc., New York 10017.

*It's Your Personality.* Rev. William J. McMahon, Brother Philip Harris & James J. Cribbin. 356 pages. 1965. Harcourt, Brace & World, Inc., New York 10017. (This and the three above are part of the Insight Series "to provide guidance for Catholic youth.")

*Look Your Best.* Candy Jones. 252 pages. 1964. Harper & Row, Inc., New York 10016.

*Love and Sex in Plain Language.* Eric W. Johnson. 68 pages. 1965. J. B. Lippincott Co., Philadelphia, Pa. 19105.

*Love and the Facts of Life.* Evelyn M. Duvall. 352 pages. 1963. Association Press, New York 10007.

*Maturity and Me.* Marion Cuthbert. 48 pages. 1963. Bureau of Communications, National Board, Y.W.C.A., New York 10022.

*Smoking and Your Life.* Alton Ochsner. 144 pages. 1964. Julian Messner, New York 10018.

*Teenage Fitness.* Bonnie Prudden. 252 pages. 1965. Harper & Row, Inc., New York 10016.

*That Certain Something: The Magic of Charm.* Arlene Francis. 159 pages. 1960. Julian Messner, New York 10018.

*The Art of Being a Girl.* Judith U. Scott. 256 pages. 1963. Macrae Smith Co., Philadelphia, Pa. 19102.

*The Girl That You Marry: A Book for Young Men about Young Women.* James H. S. Bossard & Eleanor S. Boll. 190 pages. 1960. Macrae Smith Co., Philadelphia, Pa. 19102.

*The Man That You Marry: A Book for Young Women about Young Men.* Eleanor S. Boll. 189 pages. 1963. Macrae Smith Co., Philadelphia, Pa. 19102.

*The Seventeen Book of Etiquette and Entertaining.* Enid A.

Haupt. 320 pages. 1963. David McKay Co., Inc., New York 10017.

*The Teen-Age Diet Book.* Ruth West. 180 pages. 1965. Julian Messner, New York 10018.

*What about Teen-Age Marriage?* Jeanne Sakol. 190 pages. 1961. Julian Messner, New York 10018.

*What Boys Want to Know about Girls.* Claire G. Miller. 149 pages. 1962. Grosset & Dunlap, Inc., New York 10010.

*What Girls Want to Know about Boys.* Arthur Under & Carmel Berman. 138 pages. 1962. Grosset & Dunlap, Inc., New York 10010.

*Why Wait till Marriage?* Evelyn M. Duvall. 128 pages. 1965. Association Press, New York 10007.

*You and Your Brain.* Judith Groch. 302 pages. 1963. Harper & Row, Inc., New York 10016.

*Young People and Smoking: The Use and Abuse of Cigarette Tobacco.* 96 pages. 1964. The John Day Co., New York 10036.

*Your Career—If You're Not Going to College.* Sarah Splaver. 224 pages. 1963. Julian Messner, New York 10018.

*Your College Education—How to Pay for It.* Sarah Splaver. 286 pages. 1964. Julian Messner, New York 10018.

*Your Personality and Your Job.* Daniel Sinick. 49 pages. 1960. Science Research Associates, Inc., Chicago, Ill. 60611.

*Your Teens and Mine.* Eleanor Roosevelt & Helen Ferris. 189 pages. Doubleday & Co., Garden City, New York.

## FICTION—RECOMENDED FOR TEEN-AGE GIRLS

*Candy Stripers.* Lee Wyndham. 191 pages. 1964. Julian Messner, New York 10018. (Concerns the activities of Candy Stripers, junior volunteer hospital aides.)

*The Unchosen.* Nan Gilbert. 214 pages. 1963. Harper & Row, Inc., New York 10016. (Portrays the problems of three high

school girls who suffer from the pangs of unpopularity and
what they do to overcome their difficulties.)

*Time of Understanding.* Helen J. Ferris. 206 pages. 1963. Franklin
Watts, Inc., New York 10022. (Aptly subtitled "Stories of
girls learning to get along with their parents.")

*Young Fancy.* Rosalys H. Hall. 184 pages. 1960. David McKay
Co., Inc., New York 10017. (Describes a wholesome young
girl's problems as she enters her teens.)

(*Note:* New books are published annually. Take full advantage of your school and public libraries; visit these libraries and
consult with the librarians about the latest, additional authoritative literature in this field.)

## B.  *PROBLEM PLAYLETS FOR PRESENTATION*

### THE SOCIO-GUIDRAMA SERIES

(Methods & Materials Press, 6 South Derby Road, Springfield,
N. J. 07081)

SG#1. *After High School—What?* Sarah Splaver.
SG#2. *Ma and Sue on a Job Interview.* Sarah Splaver.
SG#3. *High School Wedding Belle.* Sarah Splaver.
SG#4. *"A" is for Brother.* Sarah Splaver.
SG#5. *Mike, the Mechanic.* Sarah Splaver.
SG#6. *Late Date.* Sarah Splaver.
SG#7. *Confidence—Zero.* Milton Schwebel.
SG#8. *"But Dad, Everybody Drives!"* Jane Krumacher.
SG#9. *I.Q. High—Ambition Low.* Jane Krumacher.
SG#10. *Who's Delinquent?* David Goodman.
SG#11. *Your Friends—Who Chooses Them?* Velma D. Hayden.
SG#12. *"Granny, This Isn't 1890."* Velma D. Hayden.
SG#13. *Trust—Absent.* Sarah Splaver.
SG#14. *Shall We Go Steady?* Gertrude Forrester.
SG#15. *"Do's and Don'ts" on Dates.* Robert M. Goldenson.

SG#16. *Bottle of Trouble.* Robert M. Goldenson.

SG#17. *Jill and Perry Go Military.* Sarah Splaver.

SG#18. *"Look Who's Smoking!"* Jane Krumacher.

SG#19. *Parents Can Be Problems.* Willa Norris and Buford Stefflre.

SG#20. *Telephonitis.* Willa Norris and Buford Stefflre.

SG#21. *Timid Teen.* Willa Norris and Buford Stefflre.

SG#22. *Too Young to Date.* Willa Norris and Buford Stefflre.

SG#23. *"Every Kid's Got One."* Sarah Splaver.

SG#24. *Career Choice—When?* William H. Atkins.

SG#25. *"Cheat!"* Buford Stefflre.

SG#26. *Mama Is the Boss.* Buford Stefflre.

SG#27. *Scholarships—For Whom?* Gertrude Forrester.

SG#28. *Red Lips in the Classroom.* Willa Norris.

SG#29. *Television vs. Homework.* Willa Norris.

SG#30. *School—What For?* Buford Stefflre.

SG#31. *Love at the Lockers.* Willa Norris.

SG#32. *Disabled, True—But Able, Too!* Sarah Splaver.

SG#33. *Colored by Prejudice.* Bennetta Washington.

# INDEX

abilities, mental, 81-82
acquaintances, 139
actual self, 104-05
administrative occupations, 157-58
agricultural occupations, 155
Alcoholics Anonymous, 148
American Personnel and Guidance Association, 33
American Psychological Association, 33
amoeba, 38
anger, 91-93
anthropological factors, 37-39, 51, 103
anxiety, 95, 105-07
apprenticeships, 153
aptitudes, 83
Armed Forces, 153, 158
aspirations, positive, 176
assumed self, 104
attitudes, 49

"bad company," 134
behavior, 24, 34-37, 52, 53, 106-16, 124, 132, 134-36, 138-39 ff.
biological factors, 37-39, 40-52
blame transference, 111
Book of Proverbs, quote from, 176
brain, the, 41-52, 86
brothers. See siblings
Browning, Robert, 176
bully, 25-26

Bureau of Apprenticeship and Training, 153

car, as status symbol, 146-47
career choice, 150, 158-60, 164
character, 63-65, 104, 116, 136
cheating, 128-29
circulatory system, 35-36
clerical occupations, 155-56
college, 163, 164-66
communicating with parents, 68-69, 124. See also parents
compensation, 111-13
compulsions, 115-16
considerate person, 26-27
cortex, cerebral, 48-49
counselors, 27, 28, 32-33, 73-74, 83-84, 129, 131, 148, 149, 159-60, 162
craftsmen, 153
creativity, 49
cultural factors. See environmental factors

dating, 140-45
defense mechanisms, 106, 109-13, 115-16, 130
delusions, 115
denial, 110
digestive system, 35-36
*Directory of Approved Counseling Agencies,* 33

187

# Index

## About the Author

SARAH SPLAVER has been a noted guidance consultant and counseling psychologist for more than fifteen years. For several years she was a high school Director of Guidance. She became internationally famous as the originator of the socio-guidrama, a group guidance technique used as a means of helping young people with their problems. Dr. Splaver is a consultant to the U.S. Department of Health, Education and Welfare and has served as a consultant to many organizations. Her articles on guidance, psychology and career information have appeared in professional journals and popular teenage publications. She is the author of several books and playlets in the fields of guidance and psychology. She has lectured at conferences, young people's gatherings and parent-teacher meetings, and is the Editor-in-Chief of *Guidance Exchange,* a bi-monthly digest of recommended guidance and psychological literature.